GREAT
IDEAS
from
GREAT
PARISHES

GREAT IDEAS from GREAT PARISHES

A Parish Handbook
FROM RENEW INTERNATIONAL

Mary Ann Jeselson and
Carole Garibaldi Rogers

Liguori
LIGUORI, MISSOURI

Imprimi Potest:
Richard Thibodeau, C.Ss.R.
Provincial, Denver Province
The Redemptorists

Published by Liguori Publications
Liguori, Missouri
www.liguori.org
www.catholicbooksonline.com

Nihil Obstat:
Reverend Lawrence E. Frizzell, D.Phil.
Archdiocese of Newark Theological Commission
Censor Librorum

Imprimatur:
Most Reverend John J. Myers, D.D., J.C.D.
Archbishop of Newark

Library of Congress Cataloging-in-Publication Data

Jeselson, Mary Ann.
    Great ideas from great parishes : a parish handbook from RENEW International / Mary Ann Jeselson and Carole Garibaldi Rogers.—1st ed.
        p. cm.
    ISBN 0-7648-0990-3
    1. Parishes—Handbooks, manuals, etc. 2. Pastoral theology—Catholic Church—Handbooks, manuals, etc. 3. Lay ministry—Catholic Church—Handbooks, manuals, etc. I. Rogers, Carole G. II. RENEW International. III. Title.

BX1916.J47 2003
250—dc21   2002043286

Scripture quotations are from the *New Revised Standard Version of the Bible,* copyright 1989 by the Division of Christian Education of the National Council of the Churches of Christ in the USA. All rights reserved. Used with permission.

Printed in the United States of America
07 06 05 04 03 5 4 3 2 1
First edition

Acknowledgements

～

We interviewed many pastors, pastoral ministers, ministry leaders, and parishioners for these stories. Thank you to everyone who gave us information regarding the ideas in use in their parishes. Not every story is in this book; not every interview is recorded. At least this time around. However, we want to especially thank Ascension Church, Oak Park, Illinois; Church of the Annunciation, Paramus, New Jersey; Church of the Assumption, Morristown, New Jersey; Church of the Epiphany, Louisville, Kentucky; Church of St. Joseph, Mendham, New Jersey; Church of the Presentation, Upper Saddle River, New Jersey; Holy Family Parish, Inverness, Illinois; Holy Name Cathedral, Chicago, Illinois; Holy Spirit Church, Virginia Beach, Virginia; Notre Dame Parish, North Caldwell, New Jersey; Old St. Patrick's Church, Chicago, Illinois; Our Lady of the Holy Angels, Little Falls, New Jersey; St. Ann's Church, Ossining, New York; St. Anne Catholic Church, Oswego, Illinois; St. Brendan's, Clifton, New Jersey; St. Elizabeth Ann Seton Church, Fryeburg, Maine; St. Ignatius Church, San Francisco, California; St. Joan of Arc Church, Minneapolis, Minnesota; St. Joseph's Church, Bridgton, Maine; St. Leo's Parish, Buffalo, New York; St. Luke the Evangelist, Bruce, Mississippi; St. Mary Magdalen Church, Brighton, Michigan; St. Mary's Church, Colts Neck, New Jersey; St. Mary's Church, New York, New York; St. Monica Church, Santa Monica, California: St. Patrick Church, Rolla, Missouri; St. Peter the Apostle, River Edge, New Jersey; Spirit of Christ Church, Arvada, Colorado.

Special thanks to Jeanne Ellen Pursiano and Patrick Brunnock for their help and support and to the staff members of RENEW International for their assistance and guidance.

Contents

PREFACE ix

INTRODUCTION xi

EVANGELIZATION 1

    Welcome Everyone 1
    E-mail Outreach to Young Adults 3
    Meet the Risen Jesus Through the Eyes of a Saint 5
    I Want To Be Part of This Church 8
    Catholics Can Always Come Home 10
    I Am a Christian 13
    Reach Out to Women in Jail 16

FAITH FORMATION 19

    Teach Parents and Children Together 19
    Publish a Journal for Lent or Advent 22
    Find the Good News in Film 24
    Be "Godparents" to Teenagers 28
    Teach Us Why and How to Pray 32

LITURGY AND SACRAMENTAL LIFE 37

    Your Parents Thought So Much of You 37
    Let Children Celebrate Their Baptisms 41
    Enhance the Meaning of Marriage 43
    Make Their Wedding Liturgy Special 45
    Make Couples Feel Special in God's Eyes 49
    Welcome Into the Kingdom 52

MINISTRY 55

Enrich the Lives of Married Couples 55
Support Women Who Choose Life 57
Begin a Rural Food Pantry 59
Reach Into the Collection Basket 62
Create a Parish Garden 64
Feed the Elderly Poor 67
Create a Funeral Dinner Ministry 68
Become a Minister of Praise and Mercy 70

SOCIAL JUSTICE 75

Serve a Hunger Banquet 75
Paint a Rainbow of Hope 77
Make a Big Difference in a Simple Way 81
Build Gospel Bridges 83
Ring Out the Death Penalty 87
Care for the Stranger Among Us 91

SPIRITUALITY 97

Encourage Multicultural Devotion to Mary 97
Turn Everything Over to God 99
Show and Tell Your Family Stories 102
Share Spiritual Reading in Small Groups 105
Share Treasured Memories at Wakes 109

STEWARDSHIP 111

Share Your Dreams for Your Parish 111
What Is a Penny Worth Today? 114
Caring for God's Creation 115
Do the Right Thing 118
Many Voices, One Sunday Bulletin 120
Renew the Waters of the Earth 122

Preface

〰

From the beginning, RENEW's mission of parish spiritual renewal has been based on a simple idea: People gather together to pray, to reflect on their faith, and to determine ways to live out their faith in everyday life.

As RENEW International team members have traveled the globe assisting dioceses and parishes with the RENEW process, we have ourselves been renewed by encounters with the Holy Spirit at work in parishes in hundreds of dioceses in over twenty countries. We have come across many excellent ideas to aid the transformation of parish life.

In 2001, RENEW International launched a Web site, ParishLife.com, designed to provide online pastoral resources to parishes. As one part of our Web site, we offered a collection of Great Ideas for Parish Life—ideas that had been tried in parishes across the country and had succeeded. It is those ideas, welcomed by pastors, pastoral staff, and lay ministers, which have now become this book.

We are delighted to have this opportunity to share some of these great parish ideas and to offer practical guidelines on how you can adapt these ideas for your community. We hope you will find here the inspiration to use your own gifts to create a parish where justice and peace and love prevail.

Further ideas for transforming our parishes and communities can also be found in the variety of materials published by RENEW International in support of parishes and small Christian communities. These include *PRAYERTIME: Faith-Sharing Reflections on the Sunday Gospels*, Cycles A, B, and C; *Small Christian Communities: A Vision of Hope for the 21st Century*; and the IMPACT Series of faith-sharing booklets.

We offer our sincere gratitude to the many pastors, parish staff members, and volunteers who took the time to share their work with us.

May this collection be the first of many!

MICHAEL BROUGH
DIRECTOR, RENEW INTERNATIONAL

Introduction

∽

In California, an urban parish conducts mini summer courses in worship and prayer for its lay ministers, encouraging them to become involved in the life of the parish and to deepen their own spiritual commitment. In Mississippi, a rural mission parish of only twelve families begins a food pantry for the poor in the area. And three times a year, in suburban New Jersey, a large vibrant parish hosts welcoming dinners for new parishioners and invites them to full participation in the community.

These examples capture the spirit of this collection: more than forty practical ideas from parishes where ordinary people have come to see the connection between Sunday Eucharist and other aspects of their lives, where they act on their belief in the Christian message and transform their world.

Great Ideas From Great Parishes: A Parish Handbook from RENEW International is designed for use by pastors, parish staff, parish councils, ministry teams, lay leaders, small Christian communities—in short, all who care deeply about the life of their parish. The ideas have been gathered from across the country, from urban, suburban, and rural parishes, from large communities and small struggling missions.

We evaluated every idea according to a set of criteria:

- Does the idea help the parish and its members grow closer to Jesus Christ?
- Does the idea help draw people closer to the Catholic Church?
- Is the idea rooted in, and faithful to, Catholic tradition?
- Is the idea creative?
- Does the idea work? Has it produced good outcomes?
- Is the idea transferable?

In addition, we searched for ideas that met these additional criteria:

- Does the idea have outreach beyond the parish (to the workplace, neighborhood, town, and so on)? Does it spread the Good News to others? Does it answer the call to social justice? Does it respond in charity to a neighbor's need?
- Does the idea include global or multicultural awareness and commitment?

The familiar words from Ecclesiastes echo throughout this book: "For everything there is a season, and a time for every matter under heaven" (3:1). In the life of a parish, just as in our own lives, there are seasons; a truly vibrant Christian community recognizes and celebrates God's presence in all times and all people. Thus, you will find here some ways to celebrate baptisms and funerals; to walk with teenagers and the elderly; to care for injured humanity and to care for God's earth; to teach and to learn; to create, share, and preserve.

The book is organized around seven themes that must be a part of every parish's mission—evangelization, faith formation, liturgy and sacramental life, ministry, social justice, spirituality, and stewardship. Within each theme, you will find a variety of practical ideas from a variety of sources. We first describe each idea as it has worked in a particular parish setting. We then follow with a list of basic how-to guidelines that will help you implement a similar project in your parish. For some ideas there is further assistance in a list of resources or companion prayers and readings.

You can use these ideas in many ways. Consider the book as a catalyst for your own creativity. You can take an idea as it appears and create a replica of the parish garden or the funeral dinner ministry or the multicultural devotion to Mary we have described. Or you can change the idea, tailoring it to suit your community's identity and needs. In the how-to guidelines, we give you ways to evaluate possibilities and foresee problems when you adapt a particular idea to your environment.

This book is, first and foremost, a practical book, offering models that work and guidelines to transfer those ideas to different parish communities. But it is also, to our mind, a deeply reassuring book. Our faith is alive and well in many American parishes. These ideas are a demonstration of faith in action—faith making a difference in parish life from California to Maine.

They were developed by communities that are grounded in prayer, guided by open collaborative discussion, and diligent in their preparation for any parish effort.

Our hope is that this book not only demonstrates the vigor of some individual parishes but also fosters communication among parishes across the country. When we learn from one another, on a practical level as well as a spiritual one, we tap into the larger energy of the Roman Catholic Church in the United States, the universal Church, the communion of saints.

We are deeply indebted to all the parishes that allowed us to include their ministries in this collection. In particular, we thank the many parish staff members and lay volunteers who were endlessly patient with our persistent questions.

We are also grateful to RENEW International staff members who forwarded ideas to us, and to all those who provided wisdom, oversight, and editorial guidance. RENEW International took root in 1976 in the Archdiocese of Newark. Its unique process of bringing parishioners together to reflect and pray has facilitated healing, spiritual renewal, and greater involvement in parishes across six continents. Since its beginning, RENEW has been guided and inspired by Msgr. Thomas A. Kleissler. He was joined by Michael Brough, who became director in 2001 and who envisioned ParishLife.com, RENEW International's pastoral Web site, for which we originally researched and wrote this material.

MARY ANN JESELSON AND CAROLE GARIBALDI ROGERS

Evangelization

Welcome Everyone

W*e want to be known as a hospitable parish, a place where everyone is truly welcome," Dan Schwala says, as he explains the remarkable effort St. Monica Church in Santa Monica, California, has made to greet both newcomers and old-time parishioners at every Mass every Sunday.*

The story begins in 1994 when St. Monica Church was almost destroyed by an earthquake. Dan Schwala, coordinator of the Hospitality Ministry, says, "That was our desert experience. We had Mass in the gym for fifteen months. We would never take our community for granted again. We would welcome everyone who came through our doors in a special way because of our gratitude."

St. Monica's Hospitality Ministry now uses twelve hospitality ministers for each Mass. Their ministry begins with greeting people at the doors. Dan Shanahan, director of volunteers, says, "In our own houses we welcome visitors at the door, don't we? The liturgy is the one place where the largest group of Catholics gathers, so it's important to have ministers at the doors to make everyone feel comfortable." Before Mass, the hospitality ministers select participants for the offertory procession. They also assist with the collection and, after Mass, they hand out bulletins or stand at the welcome table.

The welcome table is another key ingredient in St. Monica's Hospitality Ministry. Tom Theisen describes the six-foot table as "literally covered with flyers about all the various activities and groups. There's not a spare inch on that table!" The welcome table is not just for newcomers, but for all parishioners, he adds, and almost every Sunday some parishioners sign up for some activity. The readings for the next Sunday and other important materials, perhaps a recent pastoral letter from Cardinal Roger Mahony, Archbishop of Los Angeles, are also available at the table.

At every Mass, the celebrant announces that hospitality ministers are available to answer any questions at the welcome table. Newcomers are invited to fill out a card with their name, address, and phone number. Another group of ministers will follow up by telephone, and the newcomers will be invited to an open house where the pastor, Monsignor Lloyd Torgerson, welcomes them and talks about the parish community.

The emphasis on hospitality has resulted in many benefits for the whole parish community. Most important, attendance at Sunday Masses has increased. Tom Theisen, who was a newcomer not so long ago and now serves as a hospitality minister two out of every three weekends, drives thirty minutes to get to St. Monica's. The church has also seen a dramatic growth in a variety of programs and ministries. Parish collections have increased, allowing the community to add parish outreach programs and give greater assistance to social service organizations in the surrounding area.

St. Monica's has made a commitment to hospitality—and to its ministers. Twice a year, Dan Schwala offers training sessions on a Saturday morning. The content is scriptural and theological; it's a time of reflection for seasoned ministers as well as new volunteers. Why are we ministers? What does hospitality mean? What can we learn from the Old Testament story of Abraham and Sarah who welcomed three strangers to their home? (Gen 18:1–15). What is the message Jesus sends us when he washes the feet of his disciples? (Jn 13:1–15).

How-To Guidelines

Here are six steps to beginning or reinvigorating the Hospitality Ministry at your parish.

- Assess your current efforts. Do you welcome people at every door at every Mass? Do your greeters see their work as "ministry"? Do they know the scriptural basis for hospitality?

- After an assessment and full discussion with the parish staff and all appropriate parish ministries, solicit volunteers for a Hospitality Ministry. Describe the new effort in the parish bulletin. Have sign-up sheets at each Mass.

- Schedule a training session for all those who are or will soon be Hospitality Ministers. Prepare carefully, allowing time for prayer, for reflection on appropriate passages from Scripture, and for discussion. Resist the impulse to concentrate solely on mechanics—who will do what, when, and where.

- Consider a welcome table in your gathering space or parish center. Begin slowly, if necessary. You may want to start by having the table open only during parish coffee times.

- Encourage celebrants to welcome newcomers and to invite everyone to stop at the welcome table.

- Don't let initial enthusiasm die; commit to a Hospitality Ministry for the long term. As St. Monica's demonstrates, the results are wide-ranging and long-lasting.

∽

E-Mail Outreach to Young Adults

Imagine receiving rave reviews from an audience of young adults. "She helps keep us connected." "The balance of spirituality, service opportunities, and social activities is just right." Read how Kristin Sadie of Holy Name Cathedral Parish in Chicago enlivens her ministry with young adults by using e-mail.

Every week Kristin Sadie, young adult minister at Holy Name Cathedral Parish, sends out an e-mail newsletter to more than five hundred young adults, single and married, living in the Chicago area.

In her work, she has found that young adults work long hours at jobs they don't always find meaningful. Many are new to the city and trying to connect to a community where they can meet others with similar values. They want to know more about their faith and be able to share that faith with others.

She decided it was important to keep in touch with these young adults, and she did it the way they do—by e-mail. She created a weekly newsletter that combines parish news with information about diocesan-wide events of interest to young people.

All issues, which are written in user-friendly language, include listings of opportunities to join faith-sharing groups, attend Sunday socials or parish happy hours, and join in service projects. Kristin uses the newsletter to relay "thank-you notes" to those who participated in works of mercy, such as collecting sweaters for people in the Philippines. And, each week, she also includes a memorable quote or fact or short poem that she finds appropriate. In one recent issue, she quoted Saint Francis of Assisi. For Holy Week, she included the words of a classic Good Friday hymn by Isaac Watts.

Steve Smith, one of the recipients of the newsletter, says that the quotes are the first things that spring to mind when he thinks of Kristin's e-mails. "They always give me a chuckle or provoke a serious thought—or give me both the chuckle and the serious thought!" Like many other young adults, Steve also appreciates this efficient way of keeping track of upcoming events.

Reaching 500 to 600 young adults weekly is an amazing achievement. Keeping them involved in their parish, active in service projects, and conscientious about their faith-life is even more of an achievement, but this effort is one that can easily be duplicated in parishes around the country.

How-To Guidelines

Here are five steps you can follow to develop your own e-mail outreach to young adults.

- Discuss the idea with the parish leadership and with active young adults in the parish.

- Determine what technical capacity you have. Does the parish have Internet access? Will you be able to use the parish address to send your newsletter and receive responses? If not, what is your alternative?

- Solicit volunteers to develop and maintain the address list.

- Solicit ideas for content. What would your particular group of young adults want to read in a newsletter? Determine frequency. Weekly? Biweekly? Monthly?

- Collect e-mail addresses at every young adult event. Publicize the newsletter in the Sunday bulletin and request e-mail addresses.

Meet the Risen Jesus
Through the Eyes of a Saint

"If she were here with us today, what would she say to us?" When the feast of their patron saint fell on a Sunday this past year, parishioners at St. Mary Magdalen Church in Brighton, Michigan, learned more about this saint—and their own relationship with Jesus.

On Sunday, July 22, the feast day of their patron saint, parishioners of St. Mary Magdalen Church in Brighton, Michigan, heard the gospel account of Mary Magdalene's encounter with the risen Jesus (Jn 20:1–18). In this full reading from John's Gospel, which is not usually heard on any Sunday of the year, Mary Magdalene lingers outside the empty tomb after Simon Peter and the other disciple return home. When a man she believes to be the gardener speaks to her, she says, "Sir, if you have carried him away, tell me where you have laid him, and I will take him away" (verse 15). Then Jesus says to her, "Mary!" (verse 16) and she recognizes him.

Father David Howell, pastor, asked people to put themselves in the scene, to consider how Mary Magdalene might have felt, what she might have thought, what she would say now about her experience. By focusing on her very personal encounter with the risen Jesus, he took the opportunity to suggest to his community that all of them should be telling the story of their own personal relationship with Jesus. The idea was "a whole new concept" for a parishioner named Diane: "I understood my relationship with God in a different way."

The story of Mary Magdalene, who is mentioned twelve times in the New Testament, second only to Mary, the Mother of Jesus, has been a source of confusion through the years. Start with her name. Mary Magdalene is the spelling used in all four gospels in the *New Revised Standard* edition of Scripture. It is also spelled Mary Magdalen, as the parishioners in Brighton, Michigan, name their patron. She is also called Mary of Magdala.

"Mary, called Magdalene" is described in Luke's Gospel as a woman "from whom seven demons had gone out" (Lk 8:2). In the gospels of Matthew and Mark, she is named among the women who stay near the cross after the men have fled, and she is named as one of the women who bring spices to anoint Jesus' body in the tomb. In John's Gospel, after her personal encounter with the risen Lord, Jesus tells her not to hold on to him, but to go tell the others about her experience. The Gospel says, "Mary Magdalene went and announced to the disciples, 'I have seen the Lord'; and she told them that he had said these things to her" (Jn 20:18).

In the very early Church, she was acclaimed as a leader, as the "apostle to the apostles," because she was the first witness to the risen Jesus and was sent to tell the others what she had seen and heard. Starting in the sixth century, when Pope Gregory I combined her story with that of the sinful woman who is described at the end of the previous chapter of Luke, the belief spread that Mary Magdalene was a penitent sinner, probably a prostitute. Over the years, artists and writers embellished that image, and it became part of our collective imagination. However, New Testament scholarship finds no scriptural basis for this tradition.

Spiritually, Mary Magdalene provides a model for modern disciples who want to understand and deepen their own relationship with Jesus and bear witness to it. Father Thomas Keating, a Cistercian monk and author of several books on contemplative prayer, writes in *The Mystery of Christ: The Liturgy As Christian Experience* (New York: Continuum, 1997), "By calling her by name, Jesus manifests his knowledge of everything in her life and his total acceptance of all that she is. This is the moment in which Mary realizes that Jesus loved her" (page 72).

Mary Magdalene is not a stranger to the community at St. Mary Magdalen Church. The parish, established in 1993, placed a five-foot statue of the saint under a skylight in the gathering space of their new parish building. The statue, by its size and placement, is meant to emphasize "her most important role—and ours." And thanks to a moving homily on July 22, 2001, many parishioners gained a new appreciation of their patron saint and a new impetus to deepen their own relationship with Jesus.

How-To Guidelines

Here are seven steps to take to deepen your community's understanding of discipleship through the life of one of the New Testament saints.

- Give your pastoral staff copies of this story from St. Mary Magdalen's Parish. Ask them what they think about doing something like this in your own parish. Get back to them about your proposal a few weeks later. Assure them that you are willing to help in any way you can.

- When you have permission to get started, ask the staff to suggest the names of six or seven other parishioners who might be interested in meeting together to work on this project. Ask for the staff's ideas about how to proceed and what saints would be appropriate.

- Call a meeting of the people who are interested. Choose your parish's patron saint or another saint in Scripture who has a special connection with your parish. You may choose a woman such as Elizabeth, Mary Magdalene, or Mary or Martha of Bethany, or a man such as John the Baptist, Andrew, or his brother, Peter. You might select one of the unnamed figures such as the man born blind in John's Gospel, Chapter 9, or the Samaritan woman at the well in John's Gospel, Chapter 4.

- Understand why you have selected this person. What does Scripture tell us about his or her life and conversion to Jesus? What can we learn from this saint to help us with our own lives? Why might this person be particularly appropriate for your community? What are the connections you want to make? Discover how he or she provides a model for modern disciples who want to understand and deepen their own relationship with Jesus and bear witness to it. You want to help parishioners to grow spiritually, not necessarily to master many facts.

- Next, select the ways you will make the connections for your parish. Consider asking the pastoral staff and parishioners to write reflections for the parish bulletin. Schedule an adult religious education session or discussion about this saint. When the Sunday readings include a passage about this person, be sure that all homilists know about the parish effort.

- Seek out help with your research efforts. Check diocesan resources and other Catholic sources for publications. As your budget allows, order videotapes or books for the parish library.

- Suggest that religious education teachers find ways to tell this person's story from the New Testament in their classes at appropriate levels. Encourage family reading of this saint's story. Suggest that families talk around the dinner table about its meaning for us today.

⟿

I Want to Be Part of This Church

"The people we met were so enthusiastic about their parish." That's how new parishioner Sharon Mahoney remembers the Welcoming Dinner she attended at Church of the Presentation in Upper Saddle River, New Jersey. Lenny DiTomaso recalls thinking, "I want to be part of this." This suburban parish reaches out to new members and gets them involved in the life of the church.

At Church of the Presentation the Welcoming Dinner Ministry draws on the talents of many parishioners in order to extend a truly hospitable greeting to new members. Three times a year volunteers organize an informal evening that begins with a relaxed sharing of hors d'oeuvres and wine, beer, or soft drinks, follows with a buffet supper, and concludes with a short program that highlights the activities and ministries of the parish.

Planning begins several weeks before each dinner as the designated volunteer chefs plan the menu and make up lists for teams of shoppers. Other volunteers send out invitations to new parishioners, who are asked to telephone a response to the parish office and to bring a "finger dessert" for the dinner. The dinner is announced in the parish bulletin for three weeks before the event.

Intensive preparation begins the day and evening before the Friday night dinner. The head chef assigns cooking tasks. Some volunteers prepare hors d'oeuvres at home; others will cook at the parish center. In the community and gathering rooms, where the event takes place, team members set up tables and create simple decorations using, for example, flowers or plants.

On Friday evening, around 6:30 P.M., all volunteers gather for a blessing. At 7 P.M., as guests arrive, some team members welcome them at the door, take the desserts they have brought, and direct them to the registration table where the pastor and other volunteers distribute nametags. As new members enter the gathering room for hors d'oeuvres, they are asked to sign a guest book. At 7:45 P.M., the buffet dinner begins. Members of the ministry team lead everyone in grace.

During dessert and coffee, ministry leaders show a series of twenty-four to thirty-six slides of parish activities. Some slides capture the community during special liturgies, such as Good Friday or First Communion, or a wedding Mass. Other slides show members of the community involved in spiritual ministries, such as teens in a prayer circle, or involved in works of mercy, such as cooking in the soup kitchen.

Three speakers—a teen, an adult, and the pastor—welcome the new parishioners. The teen and the adult speak briefly about what the community means to them; the pastor shares his experience of Presentation Parish, describing the roles of small Christian communities and of Cornerstone, the annual parish weekend retreat.

At each table, facilitators make guests feel welcome. They answer questions that arise in discussion and pass out applications for small Christian communities and the Cornerstone Retreat. The program ends by 9:30 P.M.

Donna and Jim White, who have volunteered as part of the Welcoming Dinner Ministry, are proud to be a part of the evening. Donna says, "I felt I was representing something very special and unique. I was welcoming them to my church which I have a great, great love for." As one of their guests, newcomer Sharon Mahoney clearly felt their enthusiasm and friendliness.

How-To Guidelines

Here are six steps to help you plan a Welcoming Event in your parish.

- Discuss the idea with the pastoral team.

- Determine how many new members register with the parish each year. Based on that number and the budget and the facilities available to you, determine the kind of event your community can arrange. You may prefer a Sunday brunch or a summer picnic. It is more important to do something well than to do something elaborate!

- Gather a team of volunteers. If a Welcoming Ministry does not yet exist, start one and begin to build for the future.

- Plan your event carefully. Be sure you have enough volunteer assistance to cover all aspects of the event—preparing, setting up, cooking, serving, welcoming, speaking, and cleaning up. Be creative; use the gifts present in your community.

- Decide on the program you will present. It need not include slides, but it should be informative and enriching. Enlist the presence of all groups in the parish—teens, young adults, families, and the elderly.

- Remember the focus of the evening. It is a time to be hospitable and welcoming from beginning to end. Pay attention to details like nametags and the wording of prayers. Be inclusive; be thoughtful. See Christ in all your guests.

⟿

Catholics Can Always Come Home

"God is fiercely happy to have these people back," says Gloria Biczak, of St. Joseph's Church in Bridgton, Maine, coordinator of the parish's program to encourage inactive Catholics to return to church. "It's all about what happens in the parable of the Prodigal Son."

The large white banner on the brown-shingled church says it all: "Catholics Can Always Come Home." St. Joseph's Church in Bridgton, Maine, is one of sixty parishes in the Diocese of Portland that is making a special effort to welcome inactive Catholics back to the church.

Rod Callen is someone who knows how important that welcome can be. He left the church twenty-five years ago and recently, through the program at St. Joseph's, he returned. "It's like a real void in my life has been filled," he said.

St. Joseph's began the program on the First Sunday of Lent in 2001, when the pastor, Father Bob Vaillancourt, asked all parishioners to participate by offering their prayers and Lenten sacrifices for the spiritual benefit of those who might be thinking about "coming home."

The program offers returning Catholics an opportunity to meet with one another and the team of ministers for a series of informal, open-ended discussions. At St. Joseph's, the group gathers every other Thursday evening for an hour and a half. After an opening song and prayer, the time is devoted to conversation about whatever issue people want to bring to the group. Gloria Biczak says the team often talks about the parable of the Prodigal Son, pointing out how the father prepared a feast when the son returned. "We try to tell them that Christ is running toward them now." The meetings close with a prayer and petitions.

The sessions often heal old wounds. However, sometimes people will stop in the middle of sharing a particularly painful memory and say, "I don't want to say anything more about that now." Gloria tells them, "We are all a gift from God. We can unwrap our gift and we can stop unwrapping when we are no longer comfortable."

In the first six months of the program at St. Joseph's, thirty people came to the group discussions. The team discovered that participants are in various stages of returning to church. Some returnees feel comfortable going to liturgy right away, Gloria notes. Others prefer to wait until they are ready for the sacrament of reconciliation. Some people would like to meet privately with a priest instead of attending the group sessions. Father Bob, who chooses to play a minor role in the Thursday evening discussions, sees all these people.

St. Joseph's, like other parishes in Maine that have initiated the "Catholics Can Always Come Home" program, advertises in the parish bulletin and in local newspapers. Father Bob also describes the program during the televised Sunday Mass, which is broadcast on cable TV during the week. And the banner outside the church is easily visible to passersby.

How-To Guidelines

Here are six steps to establishing a Welcome Home program in your parish.

- Consult with your diocesan offices to find out which programs they have investigated and what they recommend or may have already established in your diocese.

- Discuss various programs with the pastoral staff and lay ministers in the parish who might become members of the core welcoming team. Assess the goals of the programs, the time and financial commitments required, and the personnel and training needed for a successful program.

- Purchase necessary materials. (A list of resources follows.)

- Plan ahead. Allow time for training, for organizational meetings, for sharing the program with active parishioners, and then allow time for a strong advertising campaign to reach inactive Catholics.

- Pay attention to details that create a sense of spiritual welcome. For example, the team at St. Joseph's carefully selects appropriate prayers and music for the discussion times and also places copies of the Bible and handmade rosaries on the long table around which they gather.

- Reassess the welcoming atmosphere at all Masses and parish functions. What can you do better?

Resources

For returning Catholics, Barbara A. Smith, administrator of the Diocese of Portland's "Catholics Can Always Come Home" programs, recommends preparation via a reading list of books. Some possibilities are these:

- *Catholics Can Come Home Again!: A Guide for the Journey of Reconciliation with Inactive Catholics* by Carrie Kemp. Paulist Press (www.paulist press.com). A handbook for welcoming inactive Catholics back to membership or participation in a parish community.
- *The Essential Catholic Handbook: A Summary of Beliefs, Practices, and Prayers.* A Redemptorist Pastoral Publication. Liguori Publications, 1997.
- *Faith for the Future: A New Illustrated Catechism.* Liguori Publications, 1998.
- *The New Question Box: Catholic Life in a New Century* by John J. Dietzan. Peoria, Ill.: Guildhall Publications, 1997.

For the parish team, you might want to suggest that, for their own enrichment, team members participate in six faith-sharing sessions based on "At Home in the Catholic Church," a RENEW International booklet designed to help people recognize and appreciate the many riches of the Catholic faith, celebrate what it means to be Catholic, and grow in awareness of various dimensions of the faith. This program can be ordered by calling 1-888-433-3221 or online at www.renewintl.org/Resources/Pages/athomeimp.html.

I Am a Christian

"I cannot call myself by another name than what I am—a Christian." Who spoke these words? Read how one pastor used these words to make connections between an unfamiliar parish saint and its present community of faithful.

Making connections—among parishioners and between the parishioners and their church—is important to Monsignor Robert Slipe of St. Peter the Apostle Parish in River Edge, New Jersey. When the parish expanded its church, the pastor found documents saying that relics of Saint Perpetua are in the church's altar stone.

Saint Perpetua, a young wife and the mother of an infant son, was martyred in Carthage in the third century. She died because she would not give up her identity as a Christian, even though she understood the price she would pay—death by wild animals, viewed by cheering crowds in the amphitheater. Her name, coupled with that of her servant, Felicity, is familiar to many Catholics from the first eucharistic prayer of the Mass, which is said in some parishes on Sundays or on special feast days. Perpetua and Felicity are also named in the Litany of the Saints. But who were these women? It would seem there is little connection between their lives and the lives of contemporary Americans.

Monsignor Slipe researched the life of Saint Perpetua and found otherwise. She was a devoted mother to her son; she was a dutiful daughter until her aged father urged her to give up her faith. We have her story in great personal detail in a document entitled "The Passion of Saints Perpetua and Felicity."

This document describes the persecutions Perpetua and other Christians endured, but also tells of her personal torments as a mother until her son was allowed to remain with her in prison. Felicity, her servant, was pregnant when sent to prison; her baby was delivered there and adopted by a member of their local Christian community. Perpetua's story was finished by someone else—a witness to their deaths—who described not only the faith and courage of these two women but also their final kiss of peace.

The story of Saint Perpetua is not as remote from our lives as it would seem. Monsignor Slipe writes, "Perpetua and Felicity and their companions stand as wonderful models of faith for all of us at a time when it seems so hard to stand up for what we believe." He also suggests that Saint Perpetua can be a patron for expectant mothers, for young parents, and for grandparents "who pray for both the physical and spiritual health of their children and grandchildren."

Monsignor Slipe and pastoral associate Mary Bertani composed a prayer to Saint Perpetua (see pages 15). They then distributed to the parish a handsome fold-over card, approximately four inches by five inches, which contains a brief life of Saint Perpetua and the prayer. The cover is a beautiful icon depicting Saints Perpetua and Felicity embracing in a final kiss of peace. "There is no longer Jew or Greek, there is no longer slave or free, there is no longer male and female; for all of you are one in Christ Jesus" (Gal 3:28).

The prayer card and the homily Monsignor Slipe preached on the Sunday closest to March 7, Saint Perpetua's feast day, made important connections between the life of one saint and one contemporary Christian community.

How-To Guidelines

Here are six suggestions for enriching the spiritual life of your parish by making connections to the saints.

- Find out from those familiar with your church's history if the altar stone has relics of a saint. (Not all altar stones have relics as they are no longer required.) If necessary, you can seek diocesan help on this question.

- Discuss with the parish team why you want to draw attention to this saint. Be sure everyone understands the purpose of the effort.

- Alternately, consider focusing on the patron saint of the parish. Even if the name is familiar to parishioners, perhaps some new connections can be made to parish life today. And there are always newcomers, especially families with young children, who might welcome the information.

- Look elsewhere as well for inspiration. Perhaps the name of a street (Margaret Road) or the name of a town (Peterboro) or a city (St. Paul) will suggest a saint to you. The important thing is to draw the connection—to link a saint, a sturdy faithful "friend of God," with a present-day community.

- Once you have selected a saint, research his/her life thoroughly. You might want to solicit ideas from several parishioners, perhaps one of the small Christian communities, on how this saint's life might inspire us today.

- Request volunteers to develop ways that encourage parishioners to turn to this saint in prayer. One team might write a parish prayer; another develop and print a mini-biography; another write and schedule a children's liturgy around the time of the saint's feast day.

Prayer to Saint Perpetua

Blessed Perpetua,
we honor your presence among us in a special way
each time we look upon our beloved altar.
You knew the joys and the anguish
of motherhood and the lifelong connections
between parents and their children,
no matter the cost, no matter the pleas.
You became sister in faith to your servant Felicity,
knowing that "in Christ there is neither Jew nor Greek,
slave nor free, male nor female."
Holy Perpetua,
daughter, wife, mother, sister in faith,
we ask your intercession.
Protect all women who carry new life within them.
Guide parents and grandparents to nurture children
not only in life but in belief.
Strengthen the steadfastness of our catechumens
and of all who are new to our faith.
Encourage the constancy of catechists and teachers.
Inspire us with your own courageous spirit
and that of your sister Felicity.
And watch over this community of Saint Peter the Apostle,
as we too strive to live out the meaning
of the words "I am a Christian."

MSGR. ROBERT SLIPE AND MARY BERTANI
ST. PETER THE APOSTLE PARISH
RIVER EDGE, NEW JERSEY

Reach Out to Women in Jail

"In the beginning I was depressed knowing that these women were locked in jail for some time. But now, after twelve years, I've come to look at them as people." Rose Capazzoli and other women from her suburban parish have remained faithful to an ecumenical prison ministry.

Once a month, for more than twelve years, a group of women from Notre Dame Parish in North Caldwell, New Jersey, have visited women inmates at a county jail. The group has been dubbed the Friendly People by the inmates, but friendship is just one of the gifts they bring to the imprisoned women. Their visits, on a Monday evening, include a worship service with hymns, a reading from Scripture, a short reflection, and shared prayer. There is always time for conversation—and for doughnuts and soda.

The visitors also leave something behind, a flyer filled with Scripture verses, prayers, poems, and short real-life stories that the women can think about during the month ahead. One month, for example, they might include the Twenty-Third Psalm, the Serenity Prayer (often said as "God, grant me the serenity to accept the things I cannot change, the courage to change the things I can, and the wisdom to know the difference"), and a short reflection by Mother Teresa.

At Easter and Christmas, the Friendly People bring the inmates small packets of gifts—a washcloth, a toothbrush, toothpaste, a prayer card, or a bookmark. What's most important, however, is the commitment of the visitors. Marjorie Lucas says, "You need a really serious reason for being absent because the inmates count on seeing us. They will ask, 'Where's so-and-so?' if someone is missing."

Notre Dame Parish is one of two Catholic parishes participating in this ecumenical ministry, a work of mercy that actually began twenty years ago with Marjorie Lucas, a member of First Presbyterian Church in Caldwell. Now women from St. Peter Claver Roman Catholic Church in Montclair, St. Peter Episcopal Church in Essex Fells, and Trinity Presbyterian Church in Montclair also participate.

There are usually twelve women on the team. They visit between thirty to forty-five inmates. The visitors sit at tables in a common area, and the inmates join them there for prayer, singing, and conversation. The ministry operates with the full cooperation of the prison authorities.

The women know they make a difference in the lives of the inmates. They may arrive tired on a Monday evening, but they always leave refreshed because the women prisoners are so grateful. Marjorie Lucas says, "They don't imagine anyone remembers them."

How-To Guidelines

Here are five steps for organizing a prison ministry in your parish.

- Research prison ministry. Know what's involved. Contact diocesan offices and Catholic Charities to see what materials are available through them and which programs may be helpful to you. One online source for information is the Paulist National Catholic Evangelization Association Web site at www.pncea.org. When you're informed, discuss the idea with the parish leadership.

- Contact local facilities to determine what their needs are and who else may be visiting inmates. You might want to join an existing volunteer program rather than create a new one. Don't duplicate services unless specifically asked and don't attempt to provide services that are not welcome. Don't commit to more than your group can handle.

- Determine how this particular prison ministry will operate. What are your goals? How are these related to the needs? How many volunteers will you need? What commitment will you ask of them? Is that reasonable? Who will schedule, provide materials, and so on?

- You may want to contact other churches and places of worship in your community to see if they would like to partner with you and create an ecumenical or interfaith prison ministry.

- Invite parishioners to come to a planning meeting. Begin with a prayer to open your meeting (see the prayer that follows). Explain the new ministry. Be very clear about the goals and the commitment required. Be prepared to answer all questions fully, understanding that confusion and fear and reluctance are all possible early reactions. Have a sign-up sheet ready for volunteers.

A Daily Prayer for Justice and Mercy

Jesus, united with the Father and the Holy Spirit,
give us your compassion for those in prison.
Mend in mercy the broken in mind and memory.
Soften the hard of heart, the captives of anger.
Free the innocent; parole the trustworthy.
Awaken the repentance that restores hope.
May prisoners' families persevere in their love.
Jesus, heal the victims of crime. They live with the scars.
Lift to eternal peace those who die.
Grant victims' families the forgiveness that heals.
Give wisdom to lawmakers and to those who judge.
Instill prudence and patience in those who guard.
Make those in prison ministry bearers of your light,
For all of us are in need of your mercy! Amen.

FROM THE PAULIST NATIONAL CATHOLIC EVANGELIZATION
ASSOCIATION WEB SITE: www.pncea.org

Faith Formation

~

Teach Parents and Children Together

I n the Partners Program at Old St. Patrick's Church in downtown Chicago, parents learn about their faith at the same time as their children do—on the first and third Sundays of each month. Then, during the week, the families put what they have learned into practice through activities and discussions at home. Tana Massaro, mother of third-grader Allison, says, "I love this program. It is teaching us how to be faithful as parents."

Religious education is wrapped as a very special package at Old St. Patrick's Church in Chicago—a package that can be opened by parents and children at the same time. Twice a month, after the 9:45 A.M. Mass, families gather for religious education. The children attend classes with their peers; the parents gather with one another. One week, the parents hear a speaker address the same topic their children are studying that month; on the other week, they may join a discussion, use the library, or socialize. Once a month, there is a special family liturgy that delights and connects both children and adults.

The Partners Program, which began in 2000 as the work of Bea Cunningham, Director of Family Ministry, is organized around yearly and monthly themes. One year, for instance, the theme was "The Great Treasure Hunt." Monthly themes included "Unexpected Clues" (the Beatitudes) and "The Ultimate Travel Guide" (Jesus). Each class studied the topic in age-appropriate materials. The program included children from prekindergarten to eighth grade and ran from September to May.

Each month, Bea Cunningham and her team send home a packet of materials relating to the theme. It might include a table prayer, morning and evening prayers, or special events during the month, such as Martin Luther

King Day in January or World Food Day in October; saints for the season; monthly birthdays and parish events. Essential to each packet are the family activities and discussion ideas that enhance and deepen what children and parents are learning on Sundays. The materials for the packets come from a variety of sources.

Bea Cunningham says, "The benefit of this program is that parents totally buy into it and take their faith seriously; it's not just a Sunday activity. They live this. It really works." Tana Massaro agrees. "Partners does nice things for our family," she says.

How-To Guidelines

Here are five steps for initiating a Partners Program in your parish.

- Suggest that the pastoral team and the religious education ministry team conduct an assessment of the religious education programs at your parish. Look at the materials used, the number of children and adults involved, the results. You might want to conduct a survey among parents to determine their satisfaction with the current programs.

- Consider if your community has the necessary skills and time to develop a curriculum around themes, to produce the monthly packets, to schedule speakers for the parents. Will you need to charge a fee for the program and materials? Schedule a meeting with the religious education teachers. How would they respond to a Partners Program approach?

- If you decide to proceed, gather a team with appropriate skills. Set a time line for developing the themes and collecting materials. (A list of resources follows.) Select speakers for the parents' programs. Consult with your diocesan offices for assistance with materials and speakers. Speak to the liturgy committee about assistance in planning monthly family liturgies; be sensitive to the extra commitment this may require from a presider.

- Enlist students and parents by publicizing the new program in the bulletin and by flyers through current religious education classes.

- Send a letter to parents of enrolled students. Describe the program. Include important information, such as dates and fees. Ask for volunteers!

Resources

Here are some of the resources Bea Cunningham at Old St. Patrick's used in developing their Partners Program.

- *Share the Joy*. Woodland Hills, Calif.: Benziger. (Benziger, 21600 Oxnard Street, Suite 500, Woodland Hills, CA 91367; 818-615-2600; e-mail: Benziger@McGraw-Hill.com.) Information online at www.glencoe.com /benziger/product/child.htm#share. Each of the twenty booklets in this kindergarten program offers an opportunity for the children, the parents, and the catechist to rejoice in the specific gifts of God's love. Most of all, *Share the Joy* invites the participating families to celebrate belonging to God's family through following Jesus.

- *Celebrate Family*. Naugatuck, Conn.: Center for Ministry Development. (Center for Ministry Development, PO Box 699, Naugatuck, CT 06770; 203-723-1622; e-mail: cmd@cmdnet.org.) Information online at www.cmdnet.org. *Celebrate Family* provides an excellent way to guide families through the Church year. It is filled with reproducible activities including seasonal prayers and rituals, learning activities, popular gospel stories, service activities, and enrichment activities.

- *Family Prayer for Family Times: Traditions, Celebrations, and Rituals*, Kathleen O'Connell Chesto. Mystic, Conn.: Twenty-Third Publications. (Twenty-Third Publications, PO Box 180, Mystic, CT 06355; 800-321-0411; fax: 800-572-0788; e-mail: ttpubs@aol.com.) Also available through St. Mary's Press. Emphasizes the importance of establishing and maintaining prayer traditions in the home by offering general guidelines, specific examples, and complete prayer rituals for everyday and special occasions. Suggests ways for creating rituals for one's own family.

- *Laugh and Tickle, Hug and Pray*. St. Louis: Mo.: Concordia Publishing House. (Concordia Publishing House, 3558 South Jefferson Avenue, St. Louis, MO 63118; 800-325-3040; fax: 800-490-9889, 314-268-1411; to order: cphorder@cph.org.) *Laugh and Tickle, Hug and Pray* gives you a year's worth of weekly family-time ideas to help you share your faith together. Your family will learn to listen deeply, talk about what really matters, and reflect on God's perfect love. Your whole family will learn to relate to God and to one another.

• The Patron Saint Index at www.catholic-forum.com/saints/indexsnt.htm, part of the Catholic Community Forum; e-mail: patronsaintsindex@ hotmail.com. This site has information on patron saints and profiles of those saints.

~

Publish a Journal for Lent or Advent

Carlene Curley, a member of Young Ministering Adults in her parish, has worked on publishing Advent and Lenten Journals. These spiritual guides are both a ministry and a fundraiser. "Writing a reflection on the Gospel for the first Sunday of Advent was humbling. It brought me closer to Jesus." Read about the content of the Journals and how the young adults deepen their own spirituality by working together in this ministry.

Our Lenten and Advent journeys are spiritual adventures, times of personal growth. But it helps to have some assistance along the way. At St. Monica Church in Santa Monica, California, there are many resources for insight and information during these seasons. But two of the most popular are the Lenten Journal, produced for fifteen years, and its companion, the Advent Journal, published more recently.

The journals are the work of Young Ministering Adults, a group of singles and couples in their twenties and thirties. The Lenten Journal includes a reflection on the Gospel reading for every day of the season; the Advent Journal includes reflections only on the Sunday readings. Most of the one-page reflections are written by the young adults and often include their own personal struggles to deepen their relationship with Jesus. Meghan Howard, for example, wrote about her nephew and godson as she reflected on the real meaning of being a child of God. Elizabeth Nowicki wrote about the death of her grandmother and how it has affected her awareness of the way we spend our days. David Guiliano reflects on how difficult the practice of forgiveness is for him. "The Lord tests me every day, and I always fail at least once." As personal as they are, the reflections open outward to be of help to all who want to take their faith more seriously.

The Lenten Journal also includes information on the practices of prayer, fasting, and almsgiving, as well as recommendations for ways to show compassion, to get involved in meaningful volunteer activities, to minister to the needs of the community. The Advent Journal includes holiday recipes, regional customs, and stories of Advent traditions.

The journals, sold after all the Masses, also serve as fundraisers for the Young Ministering Adults, who are responsible for the writing, editing, cover art, and computer layout. Copies are $5 each and many parishioners buy one for themselves and additional copies for gifts. Monies collected support the outreach, spiritual, and social activities of the group.

How-To Guidelines

Here are five steps to publishing an Advent or Lenten Journal in your parish.

- With the pastoral team, discuss the spiritual materials available to your community. Is there a need for a book of reflections for the Lenten or Advent season? When will you start? For which season?

- Think about which parish group might want to take on the journal as a project. Do you have a strong Young Adults group? Or could this be a project for the Small Christian Communities? Be cautious about assigning responsibility to one person, either volunteer or staff. Producing a journal with daily reflections is a major undertaking and requires a lot of time plus a variety of skills.

- Line up a group of dedicated people with the necessary skills. You will need writers willing to contribute personal spiritual reflections, computer-literate people for data entry and layout, artists for the cover, and, finally, people to sell copies after weekend Masses and at other parish events.

- Set realistic deadlines and keep to them.

- Estimate the number of copies you might sell. Then shop around for a printer willing to give you a good price. Be sure your journal is available well before Ash Wednesday or the First Sunday of Advent. Publicize it every way you can, making particular use of parish events like retreats and days of reflection.

Find the Good News in Films

"Everybody talks about movies—what they've just seen, what they're going to see. We wanted to show people how to find the Gospel message in film." Read how a Parish Film Festival spread the Good News—and increased membership in small Christian communities.

At Church of the Presentation in Upper Saddle River, New Jersey, the small Christian communities joined together to sponsor a parish film festival. The Core Community selected six films: *Mr. Holland's Opus, Dead Man Walking, The Secret of Roan Inish, Entertaining Angels, Dominic and Eugene,* and *Spitfire Grill.* All had A-I, A-II, or A-III classifications from the United States Conference of Catholic Bishops.

The Core Community publicized the films and the dates of the screenings in the local newspaper and the parish bulletin. Each week, they set a spiritual context for the evening by opening with a prayer. (A prayer you might consider using follows in the Resources section.)

After the film, they guided the discussion with specific questions. For instance: What connections are there between the theme of the film and spirituality? What ignites your imagination to work for good or to work for change? (Other sample faith-sharing questions appear in the Sample Discussion Questions section that follows.)

For *Entertaining Angels: The Dorothy Day Story,* the organizers invited the parish Peace and Justice Ministry to cosponsor the event. They distributed copies of *The Catholic Worker,* the newspaper Dorothy Day founded in 1933, and they also gave out literature about their current ministry.

For *Dead Man Walking,* the group drew discussion points from *Reflections on Dead Man Walking*—a faith-sharing booklet in the RENEW IMPACT Series. The booklet is available online from RENEW International, 1-888-433-3221 or at www.renewintl.org/Resources/pages/reflecimp.html.

Each evening closed with a prayer drawn from the experience of the film. "After we saw *Entertaining Angels,* we prayed for the homeless and the hungry and those who provide services for the poor," said one of the organizers. "After *Mr. Holland's Opus* we prayed for families and for people with disabilities."

The festival benefitted the parish in a variety of ways. It appealed to all ages and attracted single people as well as young families to a church-sponsored event. It gave visibility to the work of the Peace and Justice Ministry. It increased parish awareness of the small Christian communities and brought new members to several groups. The Core Community had a sign-in sheet for each evening and later used the list to invite participants to future small Christian community events. (Small Christian communities are an excellent follow-up to this event.)

And, perhaps, the festival also opened people's eyes to new places where they can find the Gospel message in their everyday lives.

Sample Discussion Questions

Here are some examples of faith-sharing questions for the film, *Mr. Holland's Opus.*

- What spiritual growth do you see in the main character?

- Does the film portray family life in a positive or negative way? Give some examples for your answer. How does the film impact your view of your own family?

- How does the film portray people with handicaps? Did it change any of your own perceptions? How?

- What connections does the film make with the message Jesus brought to us?

How-To Guidelines

Here are five steps to running a Film Festival in your parish.

- Discuss the idea with the parish leadership. Investigate whether other parish ministries, such as Peace and Justice, would want to cosponsor.

- Form a committee to choose the films. Solicit suggestions; research each film; preview final selections. Consult *Our Sunday Visitor's Family Guide to Movies and Videos,* edited by Henry Herx, for plot summaries, brief

reviews, and ratings. You can also access the USCCB ratings for new releases and others from recent years at www.usccb.org/movies/index.htm,
the USCCB Web site. For more background information and issues of
interest to all moviegoers, you might want to read and then discuss "Film
Makers, Film Viewers: Their Challenges and Opportunities," a pastoral
letter written by Cardinal Roger Mahony, Archdiocese of Los Angeles. The
text is only thirty-one pages long and is available from Pauline Books and
Media, and can be ordered from Pauline Online at www.pauline.org/store
/index.html.

- Determine availability of the films in your community. Possibilities for
  rental include local libraries and local video stores. You might also consider purchasing some of the films and donating them to the parish library.

- Select dates that do not conflict with your parish, town, and local school
  calendars.

- Delegate responsibility for publicity, for hospitality, and for the program,
  which would include the selection of prayers and discussion questions. If
  you choose to follow a round-table format for discussion, invite participants from the parish or local community. Ask members of the small Christian communities to welcome people to each evening. Have a sign-in sheet
  available and set up a display table for parish information and any educational materials you think appropriate.

Resources

Here is more information to help you in planning a Parish Film Festival.

- An explanation of the USCCB ratings. The United States Catholic
  Conference's Office for Film and Broadcasting has five classifications for
  films. A-I means general patronage; A-II means adults and adolescents; A-
  III, adults; A-IV, adults with reservations; and O, morally offensive.

- Here is a brief background on the movies mentioned in the previous section.

1. *Mr. Holland's Opus*, released in 1996, stars Richard Dreyfuss as a dedicated high-school music teacher with a son who is deaf. A-II.
2. *Dead Man Walking*, released in 1995, is based on Sister Helen Prejean's book of the same name and powerfully tells the story of a woman religious from Louisiana, played by Susan Sarandon, who walks with a prisoner (Sean Penn) condemned to death. A-III.
3. *The Secret of Roan Inish*, released in 1995, is a charming Irish fantasy that reveals secrets of family life and a child's imagination. A-II.
4. *Entertaining Angels: The Dorothy Day Story*, released in 1996, is a spiritual film biography of Dorothy Day, the New York woman who advocated for the homeless and hungry, was a determined pacifist, and co-founded *The Catholic Worker.* A-II
5. *Dominic and Eugene*, released in 1988, tells the story of a pair of fraternal twins, one of whom is a mentally handicapped garbage man and the other, a medical student. A-III.
6. *Spitfire Grill*, released in 1996, takes place in a small Maine town where a young woman tries to start a new life with the help of two older local women. A-II.

• An excellent source for mini-reviews of these and other films is *Our Sunday Visitor's Family Guide to Movies and Videos*, edited by Henry Herx (Huntington, Ind.: Our Sunday Visitor Inc, 1999). It covers all movies released between 1966 and 1999 plus some earlier releases. It includes ratings from both the Office for Film and Broadcasting and the Motion Picture Association of America. You'll also find summaries of the forty-five films on the Vatican Best Films List.

• Some other worthwhile movies you may want to consider: *Life Is Beautiful* (Italian with English subtitles, 1998, A-II); *Ulee's Gold* (1997, A-III); *Babette's Feast* (1988, A-II); *The Trip to Bountiful* (1986, A-II). All of these films also provide ample opportunities for faith-sharing and discussion.

• Here, reprinted with permission from Pax Christi, USA, is a good opening prayer for a parish film festival.

For Artists, Musicians, Poets, and Film Makers

God of All Goodness,
your creative energy flows
through artists, musicians, poets and film makers.
Their gifts of art, music, poetry and films
broaden our vision to encompass beauty
that may have otherwise been missed.
Splendor is comprehended through their works
as delight is experienced in the joy of music
or the pleasure of poetry.
May the ongoing sharing of their gifts
be encouraged by
appreciative eyes and grateful ears
in a world that is in need
of loveliness and life.

CHARLOTTE ZALOT, OSB, IN *THE FIRE OF PEACE*
EDITED BY MARY LOU KOWNACKI, OSB. ERIE, PA;
PAX CHRISTI USA, 1991, P. 54.

Be "Godparents" to Teenagers

Lisa Banks says, "Being godparents to teenagers has brought my husband and me closer together, helped us parent our own kids, and made me a more prayerful person." On Sunday evenings, Lisa and her husband, Brian, open their home to ten teens as part of their parish's Godparent Program. Read more about this ministry at St. Anne Catholic Church in rural Oswego, Illinois.

The Godparent Program at St. Anne Catholic Church, Oswego, Illinois, arose as the community tried to meet the needs of their teenage parishioners. "Oswego is a rural area," says Todd Banks, Youth Minister, "and there are no Catholic high schools within traveling distance." The Godparent Program calls for adults to play a role similar to that of sponsors during Christian Initiation (baptism, confirmation, and Eucharist). It gives the parish a way to keep high-school students active in the faith, after they have made their confirmation and before they leave home for college or careers.

It is a four-year program, matching a group of teens in their freshman year with a married couple that has made a commitment to mentor the students through their four years of high school. The small groups meet every Sunday evening from September to May. Each fall, the program begins at an afternoon retreat hosted by the parish Youth Ministry and older teens. Here the freshmen have an opportunity to meet the godparent couples, to get to know them by asking questions, and then to choose which group they wish to join.

The groups then meet weekly for a two-hour session that includes prayer time, some teaching and discussion, and social time. The curriculum is fluid, up to the discretion of each godparent couple, and responsive to the needs of the teenagers. Kelly French, a junior at Oswego High School, says, "There is a lesson. But if something is bothering someone, they put aside what they have planned, and we talk." That happened, for example, after a death in the school and after the terrorist attacks of September 11, 2001.

For Scripture, the groups may use *At Home With the Word* (Liturgy Training Publications) or *The International Student Bible for Catholics* (Thomas Nelson/Word Publishing). (A list of other possible resources appears in the Resources section that follows.) The spiritual dimension also covers learning to pray, including the rosary and meditation. Todd Banks provides each couple with binders that contain suggested themes for discussion, icebreakers, and activities. And the parish offers a training program for couples who volunteer for this ministry.

Each grade level also has special programs. The freshman afternoon retreat is followed in the sophomore year by a Saturday night retreat at the parish center for each godparent group. The juniors have a weekend retreat, and the seniors end their year with a Grand Finale retreat. The sophomore, junior, and senior groups also plan and participate in a Sunday liturgy.

The program honors a teen's confidence, but also respects the role of parents in a teen's life. The godparents encourage interactive communication within families. Once a year, the godparents meet with the parents of the teens in their group. That Sunday evening the teens stay home, but during the prior week's meeting they suggest the issues to be discussed with their parents.

This year, St. Anne's Godparent Program has enrolled 125 teenagers, organized into three freshman groups, two sophomore groups, and one each at the junior and senior levels.

Lisa and Dave Van Boekel, whose oldest child is six, have been godparenting for three years. Their teens are now juniors, and Lisa says, "These kids are part of our family. They stop over in the summer even though we don't have meetings. Our kids ask, 'When are the church kids coming over?' It's been a wonderful experience."

How-To Guidelines

Here are six steps to follow in setting up your own Godparent Program.

- Assess the youth ministry programs in your parish. What are the needs of your teenage parishioners? Are there Catholic high schools in the area? How many of the teens attend a public high school? What other Catholic educational programs are available for teens?

- Consult with your diocesan or nearby parish youth ministers. What guidance or direct assistance or training materials can they provide?

- Assess the abilities of your parish staff and volunteers to run a program as demanding as a Godparent Program. Sign up enough adult couples to serve as volunteer godparents before you enroll the students.

- Schedule at least one training session for the godparents. Prepare and distribute catechetical materials. Purchase copies of *At Home With the Word* or *The International Student Bible for Catholics* or whatever other spiritual resources you choose.

- Enlist teenagers for the program by personal invitation. Reach out to them after Masses, at other youth programs in the parish, during confirmation classes. Follow up with phone calls. Be prepared to explain the program—its content and its goals—to their parents.

- Announce the new Godparent Ministry in the parish bulletin, in parish mailings and e-mailings, and at all Masses. Ask for prayers from everyone in the parish as the program begins.

Resources

- *At Home With the Word.* Chicago, Ill.: Liturgy Training Publications, 2003. (Liturgy Training Publications, 1800 North Hermitage Ave, Chicago, IL 60622-1101; 800-933-1800; www.ltp.org; e-mail: info@ltp.org.) Published yearly, this book contains the three readings for each Sunday's liturgy; a reflection on one of the readings with discussion questions; and weekly suggestions for practices of faith, hope, and charity. It also contains morning, evening, and night prayers, and seasonal psalms. The reflections and the weekly practices are appropriate for teenagers.

- IMPACT Series. Plainfield, N.J.: RENEW International. (RENEW International, 1232 George Street, Plainfield, NJ 07062-1717; 908-769-5400; www.renewintl.org; e-mail: Resources@renewintl.org.) Each of the twenty faith-sharing booklets, covering specific topics, includes material for about six sessions and can be adapted for use with teenagers.

- *New American Bible: Student Text Edition.* Nashville, Tenn: Thomas Nelson, 1990. (Thomas Nelson, Inc., P.O. Box 141000, Nashville TN 37214-1000; www.thomasnelson.com/thomasnelson/product_detail.asp?sku =0840712829.) Study edition for Catholic high-school and college-level groups; packed with helpful study features—notes, outlines, and introductory articles. Also available from local Catholic bookshops and from online bookstores.

- *PRAYERTIME: Faith-Sharing Reflections on the Sunday Gospels,* Cycles A, B, and C. Plainfield, N.J.: RENEW International. (RENEW International, 1232 George Street, Plainfield, NJ 07062-1717; 908-769-5400; www.renewintl.org; e-mail: Resources@ renewintl.org.) This resource for faith formation includes prayer, reflection, and questions for group sharing and can be adapted for use with teenagers.

- *Renewing the Vision: A Framework for Catholic Youth Ministry.* United States Conference of Catholic Bishops. Washington, DC: USCCB, 1997. 800-235-8722, www.usccb.org/laity/youth/rtvcontents.htm. U.S. Catholic Bishops address the call to personal discipleship, evangelization, and leadership for young and older adolescents. Offers a Christ-centered vision and a call to empower young people for the mission the Lord Jesus gives them. Text online in Spanish and English.

∽

Teach Us Why and How We Pray

Olga Ortega, parishioner at St. Monica Church in Santa Monica, California, says, "Last year I was on the Christmas liturgy committee and I didn't understand anything. I had no clue. Then I went to these classes and now I know why we sing certain songs, why we pray at certain times."

The idea of a hands-on mini-course in worship and prayer began with two members of St. Monica's lay pastoral team—Carol Browning, Associate Liturgy and Music Coordinator, and Delis Alejandro, Pastoral Associate in charge of the Young Ministering Adults program. The two women wanted to give their volunteers the training they needed to do a good job for the parish community. Carol Browning explains, "We've had a lot of new folks participating in our liturgies and our outreach ministries, but they don't know what to do and it's overwhelming to them."

Inspired by Cardinal Roger Mahony's pastoral letter, "As I Have Done for You," Saint Monica's encourages collaborative lay participation in its ministries. (More information about the Cardinal's pastoral letter appears in the Resources section that follows.) Carol Browning says, "The reality is that lay people need to be involved, but they first of all need to be informed." The awareness of the need for training in the components of worship and prayer services grew into a successful seven-week summer program that drew between thirty and forty people to each of the weekly sessions.

The first three sessions were devoted to prayer services, Liturgy of the Hours, the rosary, eucharistic adoration, and ethnic celebrations so popular in the community. Participants learned about the role of the presiding minister, about selecting appropriate music, and had opportunities to practice a variety of roles. The topic for the final four sessions was the Mass itself. The first session dealt with the liturgical year, explaining the lectionary cycle and the central focus on the Paschal Mystery. The second session covered the history, theology, and parts of the Mass. The third and fourth sessions concentrated on preparation for eucharistic liturgies, including both the spiritual dimension and the practicalities, such as resource materials.

The priests and lay ministers of St. Monica's presented some of the sessions. For the others, they called on specialists from the diocesan ministry office and from a local university. All presenters were asked to provide handouts—materials their students could keep for future reference. (More information is given in the Resources section that follows.)

Participants gave the sessions high marks. Trevor Rodriguez, active in the Young Ministering Adults, says, "We needed to teach people about worship and prayer. Young people don't have a good grasp of the Liturgy of the Hours. After some people attended Worship and Prayer 101, we began incorporating some of the prayers from Vespers into our regular weekly meetings."

How-To Guidelines

Here are six steps for creating Worship and Prayer 101 in your parish.

- Discuss the idea with the pastoral staff, with the religious education, adult faith formation, liturgical, youth, and outreach ministries, in particular. Suggest to all parish ministers that training in prayer and worship might enable them to better appreciate the Mass, open and close their meetings with prayer, conduct days of reflection, and deepen the spiritual dimension of their ministry.

- Decide what will be the focus of your training workshops. Do you want to focus on lay ministry during the Mass? Or do you want to develop lay leaders of prayer for other liturgical events? It is not necessary to do both at once, if your resources are limited.

- Contact your diocesan liturgical office for assistance. Ask for help in finding qualified speakers, selecting topics, and gathering training materials. You might also ask for help from the faculty of a nearby Catholic college or university.

- Review and select appropriate training materials. Make an investment in the program by purchasing copies for the parish. (Consult the suggestions listed in the Resources section that follows.)

- Schedule the sessions at a time most convenient for the majority of your parishioners. Summer evenings worked for St. Monica's; that may not work for you. Put your workshop series on your calendar well in advance, and publicize frequently in the parish bulletin. Emphasize the hands-on nature of the sessions.

- Consider running this kind of program in cooperation with other parishes. That will lessen your burden and build an even wider base of knowledgeable laity.

Resources

Here are suggestions for resources appropriate to planning and implementing these study sessions.

- "As I Have Done for You: A Pastoral Letter on Ministry," written by Cardinal Roger Mahony with the priests of the Archdiocese of Los Angeles, affirms the importance of collaborative ministry. The title, which comes from the Gospel of John, recalls the scene of Jesus washing the feet of his disciples. Jesus tells them, "You should also do as I have done to you" (13:15). The cardinal writes that the Church of today has a great need for Catholics who understand the call to service. He sees a great need for both collaboration and inclusivity in ministry and encourages a deeper cooperation between the ordained and the nonordained. Each of us must have an awareness of his or her own gifts and be willing to share them. Each of us must also be willing to recognize the gifts others bring to the table. This pastoral letter can be a fine motivating tool for ministry discussions in your parish. "As I Have Done for You" is available online at http://cardinal.la-archdiocese.org/000420.htm.

- Four books should already be available in your parish. They are official Church texts approved by United States Conference of Catholic Bishops. They include the *Lectionary, Sacramentary, Book of Blessings,* and *Rites of the Catholic Church.*

- "A Walk Through the Mass: A Step-by-Step Explanation," by Thomas Richstatter, OFM. *Catholic Update.* (St. Anthony Messenger Press, 28 W. Liberty St., Cincinnati, OH 45210; 513-241-5615; http://catalog.americancatholic

.org/product.asp?prodid=C0889.) Richstatter writes, "What does active participation mean for me when I am simply 'going to Mass' like everyone else? What happens in our lives during the week gives deeper meaning to the ritual actions we have celebrated at Mass....It is only in relation to our daily lives that the full meaning of the ritual actions of the Mass becomes clear to us."

- The Liturgy Document Series. Series of booklets published by the United States Conference of Catholic Bishops. In particular, you might want to note volume 5, General Instruction of the Liturgy of the Hours, and volume 9, Book of Blessings. Information about the booklets in the series is available by calling 800-235-8722, or online at www.usccb.org/publishing/liturgy/liturgydocs.htm.

Liturgy and Sacramental Life

Your Parents Thought So Much of You

T he letter to our daughter Megan was a touching surprise. It was a wonder-ful way for the parish to welcome her into the faith," Annie White said. She and her husband, Tom, brought Megan to be baptized at Church of the Presen-tation in Upper Saddle River, New Jersey, where all newly baptized infants re-ceive a personal letter from the community.

The 1969 *Rite of Baptism for Children* emphasizes the importance of the local community in the baptism of children. Parishes have found a variety of won-derful ways to express this ecclesial dimension of the sacrament. Here are three examples:

1. Members of the Church of the Presentation bring their babies to be baptized on a Sunday at 1:30 P.M. when all parish baptisms are scheduled. At the conclusion of the rite, the presider reads a letter from the community addressed to each infant who has been baptized. The moving personal letter, to be kept by the parents and read by the child just before con-firmation, affirms the love of God for the newly baptized baby and expresses the prayer-filled love and welcome of the community. (The source and text of the letter may be found in the Resources section that follows.)

2. At Our Lady of the Holy Angels, Little Falls, New Jersey, where baptism is celebrated within the Sunday liturgy, parents and godparents join in the entrance procession, walking in just before the presider. From the back of the church, the presider tells the parishioners that at this Mass they will

welcome a new member into the community. As they move up the aisle, the parents, carrying the baby, stop at each row and the person at the end of the row makes a sign of the cross on the baby's forehead. Father Bob Sandoz, pastor, says, "Our people love this. I wish you could see the faces of the people." The parents love it, too. Sharon and James Minnella have had two children baptized at Holy Angels. Sharon says, "We felt our whole family was welcomed and accepted." After Mass, parents and baby stand with the presider outside the church to receive the congratulations of the community.

3. Father Richard G. Rento, now retired from St. Brendan's Church in Clifton, New Jersey, added several pastoral features to the rite of baptism, as it is celebrated within a Sunday Mass at St. Brendan's. Parents, godparents, and baby join in both the entrance procession and the recession at the end of the Mass. The baby and family are included in the intentions of the prayers of the faithful; the parents and godparents take the gifts of bread and wine to the altar. At the end of Mass, just prior to the dismissal, the family is asked to step into the sanctuary and face the congregation. Father Rento holds the child up for all to see and to applaud joyfully again. The baptismal party is invited to stand at the exit of the church in an informal receiving line so that the community can see the child up close and personally express good wishes.

How-To Guidelines

Here are five steps to enhance the celebration of the Rite of Baptism for Children in your parish.

• Schedule a meeting of the pastoral staff to discuss and evaluate the current celebration of baptism in your parish. Are you doing everything you can to make the reception of the sacrament meaningful for the parents of the infant? Are you doing everything you can to involve the community in the celebration of the rite? What can you do differently—and better?

• Contact your diocesan offices for reading materials and suggestions.

• Welcome new ideas from parishioners who may have moved into the community from another parish. Allow all interested ministries to participate in the discussion.

- After decisions have been made, describe the changes to the entire community. Use the opportunity for catechesis, giving all parishioners an opportunity to reflect on the importance of their own baptism and their commitments as Christian disciples.

- Be sure to incorporate the changes in the materials presented to expectant parent(s) when they inquire about baptism.

Resources

Here is additional information on a parish letter to newly baptized infants.

Father Ken Evans first learned about the parish letter to newly baptized infants from Father William J. Bausch, who was pastor of St. Mary's Church, Colts Neck, New Jersey. Father Bausch's pastoral ideas for the celebration of baptism, including his version of the letter, appear on pages 49 through 54 of his book, *The Total Parish Manual: Everything You Need to Empower Your Faith Community* (Mystic, Conn.: Twenty-Third Publications, 1994). At St. Mary's, where baptisms take place during the noon Mass on the second Sunday of the month, the letter is read to the entire congregation at the end of Mass, in place of the usual meditation time after communion.

Here, used with permission, is the text of the letter given to the parents of newly baptized infants at Church of the Presentation, which differs in some details from that used by Father Bausch at St. Mary's. Use the sample as your model and make modifications to suit your parish community and your celebration of the rite.

Dear [fill in child's name],

Several years ago your parents thought so much of you that they wanted to share the most precious gift they had—their faith. So they approached the Christian community of the Church of the Presentation in Upper Saddle River, New Jersey, and asked the people if they would be willing to create a climate in which you could grow to know and love Jesus Christ.

The community said yes, and so on Sunday, [fill in date], *you and your parents, godparents, family, and friends came to Presentation and there you were welcomed into the Christian family.*

The people present were happy and they applauded you afterward; then your parents brought you home and had a celebration there, too, because of this joyful event. That was some years ago.

Now we hope that you have been raised in the faith and know how much God loves you and how happy God is to have you as his child. For no matter what happens to you in life—no matter who hurts you— God will never stop loving you. Even though—like the rest of us—you sometimes make mistakes, once God sets his heart on you, he will never let you go. God promised this at your baptism, and God always keeps his word.

We hope, therefore, that this letter finds you well. Signing this letter is the priest (or deacon) who baptized you. Your parents, godparents, members of your family, and friends have also signed this letter. The host couple from Presentation has also signed the letter. They were part of the parish that first formed your Christian family and first welcomed you into their midst.

All of us at that time gave you a hearty welcome. Today as you read this and prepare for your confirmation, we still wish you well, pray for you, hope for you, and through the years—and perhaps the distance— we still love you.

God bless you!

Presider: _____

Host Couple: _____

Parents: _____

Godparents: _____

Family and Friends: _____

Let Children
Celebrate Their Baptisms

"This is a chance for the children to renew the baptismal promises someone else made for them. Today, they make their promises for themselves." Each year, Father Jack Wahl welcomes the children of his parish, Old St. Patrick's Church in downtown Chicago, to a Baptism Jubilee. Read how the children gather around the baptismal font and participate in the liturgy that day.

Three years ago, the parish of Old St. Patrick in downtown Chicago installed a new baptismal font when the renovation of the back of the church was completed. As the parish planned a celebration and blessing of the new font the Family Ministry Team—and in particular, the baptism ministry, led by Jeanne Phenany—wanted to make the event special for the children. They recognized that most of us are baptized when we are babies and that children should have an opportunity to claim belief in Jesus and membership in the Church for themselves.

The celebration was so successful that the parish now repeats its Baptism Jubilee every year. The special liturgy takes place at the 12:45 P.M. Mass on the Sunday closest to the feast of the Baptism of the Lord. After the homily, the children, from preschool age through early teens, gather around the baptismal font. They are encouraged to bring their own baptismal candles to church, but the Baptism Ministry Team supplies tapers for those who do not have their own candles. The children—and the adults—light candles and repeat their baptismal promises. The presider gathers with the children at the baptismal font and explains to them the meaning of what they are doing.

The team tries to include children in many of the ministries for that Mass. They serve as greeters, ushers, readers, and gift bearers.

The Baptism Jubilee is described in the parish bulletin for several weeks before that Sunday. The team sends out flyers to students at the parochial school and to students in the parish's religious education program.

After the Mass, the church sponsors a reception, serving coffee and juice with child-friendly cake to all guests.

Eileen Durkin, whose daughter Nora has participated in the Baptism

Jubilee for the last three years, thinks the celebration keeps her five children connected to their faith. "From a parent's perspective," she says, "it's a wonderful way to make the sacrament of baptism a continuing part of their lives." Annette Buys, the mother of two boys, ages eleven and fourteen, adds, "My son liked being around the baptismal font. It was a new experience for him. I think it helps the children get an idea of their baptism, which they can't remember."

How-To Guidelines

Here are six steps for celebrating a Baptism Jubilee in your parish.

- With the pastoral team, consider what efforts your parish currently makes to raise awareness among both children and adults of their baptismal promises. How would your particular community welcome a Baptism Jubilee at one of your Sunday liturgies?

- Consider celebrating, as Old St. Patrick's does, on the Sunday in January closest to the feast of the Baptism of the Lord.

- What components do you want to include in your celebration? Look at the curriculum of your religious education programs. How can you reinforce lessons being taught there?

- Be sure you understand liturgical guidelines for the celebration of the Eucharist, and always work within these. See the 2000 Revision of the *General Instruction of the Roman Missal,* www.usccb.org/liturgy/current /romanmissalind.htm.

- Encourage wide attendance by reaching out to children in the community through all available means—for example, parish bulletin, flyers, e-mail, religious education classes, confirmation classes, parochial schools, and so forth.

- Welcome everyone with coffee or juice and child-friendly cake after the Jubilee.

Enhance the Meaning of Marriage

"We went because we were curious," Terry Mironenko says of the Wedding Preparation Weekend at Church of the Presentation in Upper Saddle River, New Jersey. "But we loved it. We had a chance to talk about things you might never discuss before marriage." This parish provides spiritual and emotional support for couples planning to marry.

Three times during the year, the Church of the Presentation in Upper Saddle River, New Jersey, invites couples who will be married in the parish to a Wedding Preparation Weekend. Attendance at a weekend is optional and in addition to the required pre-Cana program. Still, Presentation Parish has had great success with Wedding Weekends. Twelve to fifteen couples attend each weekend.

Terry Mironenko and Matt Brogan were as busy as other couples in the weeks before their wedding ceremony, but they took time out for what Terry called "concentrated interaction between us." And they found the weekend had many benefits. They talked about family values and finances—areas they might otherwise never have discussed. And they met other couples going through the same experiences. Terry says, "It was a very positive experience, very different from pre-Cana."

On Friday evening, designated Music Preparation Night, three members of the parish team, Edward Ginter, Director of Music, Peggy Gelnaw, Assistant Director of Worship, and Carol Reilly, Parish Wedding Coordinator, help the couples envision and plan their wedding ceremony. The team compares the components of a Nuptial Mass with those of a wedding ceremony not in the context of a Mass. They review the options for Scripture readings.

Most of the evening is devoted to showcasing the vocalists and instrumentalists who are available for parish weddings. The musicians provide examples of processionals and recessionals, responsorial psalms, communion songs, and other musical selections that are available. The couples are invited to note their choices and contact the musicians directly. Peggy Gelnaw distributes contracts and the couples are instructed to mail a contract to each musician they select, as well as to the parish office.

On Saturday, the couples are invited to participate in a daylong workshop for the engaged. It's a day to stop worrying about fittings, limousines, invitations, and seating charts. In a series of short presentations by Dennis Corcoran, Director of Worship, and Maura Roem, Director of Family Life Ministry, the couples are encouraged to look at issues that could cause conflict in their marriage. They are given time to discuss topics which include finances, differing family traditions, fair fighting, and alternate ways of resolving conflicts. The day concludes with the 5 P.M. liturgy.

On Sunday, Presentation offers a brief wrap-up session with Dennis Corcoran. He puts the wedding liturgy in perspective, weaving in some bits of history and explaining common symbols such as the aisle and the wedding ring. (The aisle symbolizes the couple's journey into new life; the ring is a symbol of their eternal love.) His focus is on the liturgy itself—what makes it authentic, what it should convey to the couples, to their families, and their guests.

In one suggestion, for instance, he asks the bride and groom to memorize their vows. "It's just three sentences," he tells them, "and it helps everyone understand that you confer the sacrament on each other."

Church of the Presentation is a large parish and could easily have lapsed into a "wedding factory." Instead, with careful planning and warm hospitality, they have enhanced the meaning of the sacrament for bride and groom and provided spiritual sustenance that may last well into the future of many marriages.

How-To Guidelines

Here six steps to organizing a Wedding Preparation Weekend in your parish.

- Consult with the parish leadership, especially those in liturgical and music ministries. Schedule a meeting for all those who might be able to assist in planning or implementation.

- Discuss the specific needs of young couples in your community and the services you can offer as a parish team. Develop your own goals and objectives for the program. Do you want to focus on just the wedding liturgy? Or do you want to include a marriage component? Will the weekend enhance or compete with pre-Cana programs?

- Be flexible. If, for instance, you have limited staff, you may be able to accomplish your goals in a one-day program. Consider joining with other nearby parishes to offer the Music Selection Night. Ask your diocesan/archdiocesan office for assistance with presenters trained in wedding liturgies.

- Be sure to plan far in advance. Put the Wedding Preparation Weekend on the parish calendar and publicize it early and often.

- Solicit feedback from the young couples who attend the first weekend. Make adjustments. Build for the future.

- Invite some young couples to come back, after they are married, to work on the team.

~

Make Their Wedding Liturgy Special

"The letters we wrote to each other—and that Deacon Mike read at the wedding—gave us an opportunity to reflect on our love and gave everybody there some insight into who we are. The Blessing of the Hands was special because it made us think of the future." Courtney Heffelfinger describes two of the special touches Deacon Mike Hanly incorporated into their wedding liturgy.

Church of the Assumption in Morristown, New Jersey, is such a beautiful church that parishioners and non-parishioners ask to be married there. The priests and deacons often do not know the couples well. The parish has compiled a list of several ways couples and clergy can work together to enhance their wedding celebration. Here are two of their best ideas:

Homily Letters

The priests and deacons strongly urge the engaged couples to write letters to each other. In the letters, the couples describe why they love and want to marry each other. The couples do not exchange the letters but give them to the priest or deacon who will perform the wedding ceremony. He then has an opportunity to weave excerpts from the letters into his homily. When

Deacon Mike speaks of the importance of commitment, how it transcends love and friendship, for example, he quotes from the letters. "I read the letters slowly with emotion. I look at the bride or the groom, and invariably the bride will start to cry and the groom wells up with tears. It's a very moving moment." Reading from the letters provides a deeply personal message for bride and groom. But it also pleases the guests who feel as if they get to know the couple better. At the end of the homily, the celebrant offers a prayer for the bride and groom that emphasizes the theme of commitment. (A prototype of this prayer appears in the Resources section.)

Blessing of the Hands of the Bride and Groom

After the vows have been said and the rings exchanged, the priest or deacon reads a special prayer for the newly married couple. It is a very appropriate time to bless the hands of bride and groom; they have just placed rings on their fingers. This prayer describes how their hands will support each other through life's joys and sorrows, in times of love and pain. It also speaks of the difference these four hands can make in the world. As he reads the prayer, the celebrant quietly instructs the groom when to take the bride's hands in his; when she should take his in hers; and when they both hold the other's hands. Geoff Marino and his wife, Jessica, have great memories of the Blessing of the Hands at their wedding. Geoff says, "It was an intimate moment. It gave us a chance to reflect on what was really happening while we were holding each other's hands." (The text of the Blessing of the Hands of the Bride and Groom appears in the Resources section that follows.)

How-To Guidelines

Here are five steps to suggesting and implementing these additions to wedding liturgies in your parish.

- Discuss these two suggestions with the pastoral team, including the deacons. Ask for feedback. Do they believe the letters will help in homily preparation? Will they be comfortable reading excerpts aloud?

- Make copies of the prayers for distribution and comment. Revise if necessary to suit your parish community and the couples who are married there.

- Be sure that priests, deacons, and any ministers who meet with engaged couples understand the value and meaning of these suggestions and are able to convey them to the couples.

- Request the letters from bride and groom well before the ceremony. Settle on a time frame that everyone on the team can comfortably use. This will minimize confusion. For instance, do you want the letters from the bride and groom to be sent to the priest or deacon three weeks before the wedding? Or do you prefer a month?

- Compose typed information sheets to be distributed to the engaged couples explaining their responsibilities. Be sure the priests and deacons have an information sheet—and the final version of the prayers—for their use.

Resources

Here are sample texts for the two special additions to include in the Wedding Liturgy.

Blessing at the End of the Homily

Since you have decided to commit yourself to each other in front of God, God now sanctifies your relationship in the sacrament of matrimony. Therefore, I now pray that your sanctified, committed relationship is successful on three levels:

On the spiritual level, I pray that your sanctified, committed relationship is always based on God's love and guided by God's Word.

On the physical level, I pray that your sanctified, committed relationship is always open to the possibility of being involved in God's procreative process, and that God blesses you with healthy and happy children.

On the emotional level, I pray that in your sanctified, committed relationship, God will deepen and nourish, through the years, the love and friendship that you share today.

Blessing of the Hands of the Bride and Groom

As the groom takes the bride's hands, the celebrant says:

> These are the hands that hold yours today, your wedding day, as she pledges her love to you and accepts your ring. These are the hands that are smooth and young and carefree now, but will become lined and rougher in the years ahead. These are the hands that, God willing, will hold you in joy and excitement each time she says you are having a child, and that together you have created a new life. These are the hands that through the years will caress your body in the passion of love. These are the hands that will tenderly hold your face and wipe tears from your eyes in wonder and awe that you would cry for her.

As the bride takes the groom's hands, the celebrant says:

> These are the hands, young and strong and vibrant with love, that hold yours today, your wedding day, as he promises to love you all the days of his life. These are the hands that will one day caress your body to make the passion of love come alive in you. These are the hands that will countless times wipe tears from your eyes, tears of sorrow and tears of joy. These are the hands that will comfort you, when fear or grief racks your mind. These are the hands that will tenderly lift your chin and brush your cheek, as they raise your face to look into his eyes, eyes filled completely with his overwhelming love for you.

As the bride and groom hold each other's hands, the celebrant says:

> These are the hands that celebrate the sacrament of matrimony. These four hands are part of God's plan. These hands can reach out to the lonely and discouraged, bring hope to the destitute, heal the abused and hurting children of the world, and teach your friends the wonders of married life. These four hands are the hope of a troubled humanity. For these are the hands that can change the world. God bless you today and each day of your married life.

Make Couples Feel
Special in God's Eyes

"It's the most wonderful gift for couples. It hits you in a place you forget you had." Camille Caminiti speaks for herself, her husband, Paul, and many other couples who have celebrated their wedding anniversaries with a special Mass and anniversary dinner at Church of the Presentation in Upper Saddle River, New Jersey. Read how this parish makes married couples of all ages feel special in God's eyes—and in their own.

Once a year, for the past nine years, Church of the Presentation has honored its married parishioners who are celebrating a special anniversary with a Mass and anniversary dinner. Those who have participated agree on one thing: it is a memorable experience—almost as memorable as their wedding ceremony itself.

Planning for the June event begins with two winter meetings of the Core Team. These are the parishioners who will oversee every detail of the evening from the invitations to cleanup and who serve in this ministry for more than one year. In the spring they will be joined by another group of parishioners—last year's honorees who have volunteered to help another group celebrate this year. All the planning sessions and the event itself emphasize the spiritual dimension of marriage.

Coordinators Barbara and Denny Foley begin meetings of the Core Team and the full Celebration Team with prayer and a reading from Scripture, followed by a faith-sharing question. All are carefully chosen to deepen the faith and commitment of spouses. Barbara reports that participants feel closer because of the sharing they do at the meetings. Some examples of faith-sharing questions used at Presentation appear in the Resources section that follows.

The Mass, which includes a renewal of the marriage vows, is filled with prayers, readings, and songs that deepen the marriage commitment. There are other special touches, too. The Celebration Team attends the liturgy, but they sit in the choir loft, leaving the body of the church for the honorees. At the end of the Mass, as the honorees leave the church and walk to the reception and dinner in the parish center, Celebration Team members line the corridors and applaud them. One volunteer notes, "The couples, both men and women, are very touched by the tribute. Many of them are filled with tears."

Careful attention to details makes the reception and dinner as memorable as the Mass.

- At the reception in the gathering room, which precedes the dinner, tables display wedding pictures of the couples.

- At the dinner in the community room, couples celebrating the same anniversary sit together. Each table, decorated with tulle, ivy, candles, and photographs of the couples, has as its centerpiece a special wedding cake made by parishioners.

- During the dinner, a musician, who receives musical selections from the couples via the Core Team, plays different wedding songs, announces couples by name, and asks them to dance their song.

- Parishioners skilled in photography take pictures of each couple in a specially decorated niche where they sit on a park bench surrounded by flowers. The photographs are given to the couples as a gift; they also receive a pair of goblets with the date engraved.

Barbara Foley sums up the experience for the Celebration Team. "It's an easy, happy ministry," she says. "We're preparing for a big party. The volunteer couples who were honored last year are eager to give the same experience to others." Her husband, Denny, adds, "The smiles on the couples' faces throughout the evening make all the preparation more than worthwhile."

How-To Guidelines

Here are six steps to initiating a Wedding Anniversary Mass and Dinner in your parish.

- Discuss the idea with the pastoral team. Solicit parishioners to serve as coordinators and as members of the Core Team. They will be responsible for all planning from invitations to cleanup. Emphasize that the event should have a spiritual dimension, as well as a festive atmosphere.

- Select a date many months ahead; put it on the parish calendar. Place an announcement in the parish bulletin several months before the event. Ask parishioners who are celebrating a special anniversary to notify the parish office so that they will receive an invitation to the event.

- Be sure to involve the parish liturgist and musician in planning the Mass. Print up a booklet to distribute to all the couples. It should include the words to the songs, the readings, the prayers, and the vows.

- Divide up responsibilities for the reception and dinner according to the kind of event you plan (formal or informal) and the gifts your parishioners can offer. Some of the areas you will want to remember are invitations and nametags, decorations, food preparation and serving, photography, music, and cleanup.

- Remember that for the first year you will not be able to count on extra volunteers from among the prior year's honorees. Plan ahead; ask for volunteers for next year's event at this year's dinner.

- Have fun. Celebrate!

Resources

Here are some faith-sharing questions the Celebration Team at Church of the Presentation used when they met to plan the Anniversary Mass and Dinner.

- After a reading of Ephesians 5:25–32, the passage that begins, "Husbands, love your wives, just as Christ loved the church and gave himself up for her…," couples were asked to "share a time when I recognized and appreciated my spouse as the most important person in my life."

- At one meeting, a litany-type prayer emphasized the gifts of each spouse. To each segment, couples were asked to respond, "Thank you for all your blessings, Lord." After the prayer, couples shared with the group stories about how they met.

- At another meeting, couples were asked to consider the question: "What good quality have you taken on as a result of living with your spouse?"

- And another question: "Share with someone else the quality that attracted you to your spouse." Later, in the large group sharing, spouses would hear each other's responses.

~

Welcome Into the Kingdom

Sometimes it takes only a small touch, some sign that the parish cares, to comfort mourners at a funeral. Here's how one parish created a banner that can be personalized for each funeral, enhancing the celebration of the Mass of the Resurrection and consoling those who mourn.

Roseanne Russomagno considered her mother to be her best friend, and she knew how difficult the funeral would be. "On the day of my mother's funeral, we walked into the church and saw a lovely banner with my mother's name, Flora, on it, welcoming her into the kingdom. My family and I felt we had come home to where we belonged. And we knew my mother was all right."

The personalized banner has comforted many other parishioners at Notre Dame Parish in North Caldwell, New Jersey. Credit for the idea goes to the pastor, Monsignor Edward Ciuba, who saw a similar banner at a funeral in Florida. Notre Dame's banner was designed and sewn by Sister Carol Jaruszewski, RSM, Mrs. Lee Rubino, Mrs. Ruth Shiever, and Mrs. June Schott.

The banner, which measures approximately four feet by six feet, is suspended by a white cord from a portable stand. At Notre Dame it is placed next to the baptismal font, which is in the front of the church. The casket is wheeled into the church and placed next to the font and the banner; the pall is placed over the casket; and the casket is then brought to the front center aisle. The banner is visible throughout the liturgy.

The words on the banner are "Welcome [space for deceased's first name] into the kingdom prepared for you." This banner is made from a white upholstery-weight fabric, hemmed on all sides. An extra piece of the same fabric was slip-stitched into a space below the word "Welcome" so that the name, which is changed for each funeral, is not pinned directly onto the banner. A calligrapher drew the letters of the permanent words on the banner and a parishioner skilled in crewel embroidery sewed them on.

In addition, along the left side and top of the banner a vine is included in the design of the banner. The vine is an appropriate visual image for funerals, recalling the words of Jesus, "I am the vine, you are the branches. Those who abide in me and I in them bear much fruit" (Jn 15:5). For Notre Dame's banner, the vine was first painted with acrylics on muslin, then cut out and pasted on the fabric.

The letters of the name of the deceased are cut from felt. Notre Dame's team made two sets of each capital letter and three or four sets of lowercase letters so they could accommodate any name. The letters are stored with the banner and attached before the liturgy by one of the ministers assisting at the funeral.

Notre Dame has found a wonderful way to bring a small measure of comfort to mourners—and to involve more parishioners in the ministry of consolation.

How-To Guidelines

Here are five steps to creating a Welcome into the Kingdom banner for funerals in your parish.

- Consult with your pastor, the liturgy committee, and any other appropriate ministries. Be sensitive to the culture of your parish. Understand or seek advice on the liturgical guidelines for Christian funerals.

- Decide where and how you will place the banner in the church. Will the parish need to purchase an appropriate stand? Where is the baptismal font located? Does your parish place the paschal candle near the casket?

- Recruit volunteers to design, paint, and sew the banner. Estimate costs and seek approvals from the pastoral team before purchasing materials and beginning work.

- Follow Notre Dame's suggestions or create your own banner, using images, colors, and lettering that are in keeping with the liturgy, but also appropriate for your parish and its particular character.

- Describe the banner—and thank the volunteers who worked on it—in the parish bulletin. You may want to schedule a blessing of the banner before it is first used at a funeral.

Ministry

~

Enrich the Lives of Married Couples

*H*arry and Linda Tourville have three children, two of them teenagers, and they were so busy they were forgetting how to do things as a couple. "We didn't want to become strangers under the same roof," Harry says. Date Nights have helped them—and more than 100 other couples from their parish—reinvigorate their marriages.*

Marilyn and Tom Kortendick, leaders of the Marriage Enrichment Ministry at Holy Family Church, Inverness, Illinois, brought Date Night to their parish in 2001. Marilyn had attended the annual conference of the National Association of Catholic Family Life Ministers and brought back the book, *Ten Great Dates to Energize Your Marriage*, by David and Claudia Arp. With their pastor's enthusiastic support, the Kortendicks and a team of three other couples planned and scheduled a series of Date Nights for parish couples, one a month for ten months.

At Holy Family, participating couples purchase the book from the parish and are asked to read a chapter before each date. (More information on the book, training materials, and videos appears in the Resources section that follows.) On the scheduled Friday, all couples gather together at 7 P.M. in the church. A brief prayer, usually led by Father Patrick Brennan, the pastor, begins the evening. The Marriage Enrichment team then shows an appropriate video and, by 7:30 P.M., each couple leaves for a date at a local restaurant. And each brings along a worksheet dealing with that month's topic, which will help focus that night's conversation. After they've ordered their meals, they fill out the worksheet and during dinner they discuss what each has written.

There are a few rules for these evenings. Couples are not supposed to eat with other couples. These are dates for two. They are not supposed to discuss the children, their work, or their finances. They are to dwell on the positive in each other and in the relationship.

The Holy Family team provides some support services for dating couples. For example, the parish runs a nursery from 6:30 to 9:15 P.M. for parents who can't get sitters for a Date Night. The team also contacts the Chamber of Commerce to arrange discounts for restaurants and offers coupons to couples who request them. Each month, they raffle off two ten-dollar gift certificates to a local pizza place.

Date Nights began with close to 150 couples participating. During the course of the ten months, as couples found difficulty in attending one or another Date Night, the parish encouraged them to read the chapters on their own and then go out to dinner whenever they could. The parish also purchased an extra set of videos and made them available for couples to borrow, view, and return.

Linda Tourville says, "We had forgotten to keep dating while we were married. I've recommended the program to others. I really enjoyed it."

How-To Guidelines

Here are five steps for starting Date Nights in your parish.

- Discuss the idea with the pastoral team and with other appropriate ministries in your parish.

- Order a sample copy of *Ten Great Dates to Energize Your Marriage* and review it carefully. (Ordering information and a brief review of the book and related training materials appear in the Resources section that follows.)

- Evaluate the program in the context of your parish community. Will this type of program, with an ongoing commitment, be welcomed by your parishioners? Can you offer support services? Are some nearby inexpensive restaurants available?

- Write about Date Nights in your parish bulletin. Invite interested couples to come for an organizational meeting. Discuss the frequency and timing of the Dates. Once a month, as Holy Family has done? Twice a month? Find out where you will need to provide support services and where you will need additional volunteer help. Order books and videos only after you have assessed the level of interest and commitment among parish couples.

• Put all dates on the parish calendar; invite the pastor to offer the opening prayer. Publicize the program in neighboring parishes and to other churches and houses of worship in your area. Catholic couples are not the only ones who benefit from attending Date Nights.

Resources

Ten Great Dates to Energize Your Marriage by David and Claudia Arp. The book contains ten short chapters, one for each date, plus His and Her copies of the worksheets for each date. Each chapter covers a different topic, such as "Resolving Honest Conflict" or "Balancing Your Roles As Partner and Parent," and each chapter provides both advice and numerous examples from the authors' own marriage, as well as their work with others in marriage seminars. For example, in "Resolving Honest Conflict," which is the subject for Date Three, the Arps explain inappropriate ways of handling conflict, then look at the ways we express our feelings, and finally lead into appropriate ways to resolve conflict. The worksheets engage the couples in a discussion of these topics.

The book, a facilitator's training manual, and accompanying videos are also available. For more information, prices, and ordering information, go to www.marriagealive.com.

∿

Support Women Who Choose Life

"We can say we're against abortion, but if we're not going to support women who choose life for their babies, then our words are meaningless." Marlene Miller from Church of the Epiphany in Louisville, Kentucky, describes the reason her parish gives a Baby Shower every Mother's Day and donates all the gifts to local women who have chosen life, but need help.

The Mother's Day Baby Shower, which Church of the Epiphany began eight years ago, is just one part of the parish's Respect Life efforts. Sister Chris Dobrowolski, IHM, on the pastoral team, says that the parish has an active Social Responsibility ministry and a consistent Respect Life ethic, opposing both abortion and the death penalty, and extending help for women who are abused.

Marlene Miller, who serves on the Respect Life subcommittee, coordinates the annual Baby Shower. "We begin two or three weeks before Mother's Day," she says, "by sending invitations to the shower home with the children in our Religious Education program. We also put an announcement in the bulletin and a poster in the church's gathering area." All parishioners are invited to come to the shower and bring baby gifts. At the same time the committee places a white mini-crib in the gathering area where people who cannot come to the shower leave their gifts. Checks are welcome, Marlene Miller says.

On Mother's Day, the party is short but festive, scheduled between two morning liturgies. The committee serves orange juice, coffee, muffins, and a cake—just like those served at other showers. About 200 parishioners attend and leave their gifts in the crib.

The committee distributes the gifts through Opportunities for Life and Mother Infant Care, two local Catholic efforts that assist pregnant women in need.

Opportunities for Life is a 24/7 crisis hotline funded by the Catholic Conference of Kentucky. Callers are treated with respect, given a chance to tell their story, and talk through their problems. The volunteer listeners are trained to be non-judgmental and to offer appropriate assistance. They counsel the callers through life-affirming decisions, offering them information on adoption or on parenting. Lyndee Rouchelle, director of the hotline, says, "We want callers to feel God's love through us."

Mother Infant Care is a five-week parenting course for pregnant women in need. The women receive instructions in such topics as prenatal care, infant care, car seat safety, and so on. For each week the women attend the classes, they earn a specific gift, such as a digital thermometer, a receiving blanket, or some personal care products for themselves. At the end of the course, each woman receives a check to be used for a baby crib and mattress. Helen Rothgerber, who runs the program for the Diocese of Louisville, says, "These women have no support, except through Mother Infant Care. We teach them necessary skills. But we couldn't do this without the parishes, without the people from Epiphany."

How-To Guidelines

Here are five steps to organizing a Respect Life Baby Shower in your parish.

- Survey the needs in your area. What are other churches and agencies doing to assist pregnant women in need of emotional, psychological, or financial support? What needs are still unmet?

- Consult with the pastoral team and your diocesan ministry teams. Find out how a baby shower would fit into parish and diocesan Respect Life initiatives.

- Schedule an organizational meeting for an appropriate committee or open it to anyone from the parish. Be prepared to present all the basic information people will want to hear. Know, for example, where the gifts will go and what will be expected of volunteers.

- Select a date. Consider Mother's Day, but be open to other arrangements that may be better suited to your community. Assign volunteers to send out invitations, prepare refreshments, and deliver the gifts you collect to appropriate agencies.

- Publicize the event. Use press releases, inserts in the parish bulletin, and announcements from the pulpit.

~

Begin a Rural Food Pantry

"We have come to understand what it means to be the Body of Christ. We are his hands and his voice." In economically depressed rural Mississippi, a tiny mission parish of only twelve families has begun a successful food pantry to help the poor in their area. Read about Our Daily Bread at St. Luke the Evangelist Church in Bruce, Mississippi.

The story begins in 1999 when a Baptist woman from Bruce approached some of St. Luke's parishioners and suggested a joint effort to help get food to the poor in the area. In Calhoun County, there are sixty Southern Baptist churches. Tiny St. Luke's, with regular Sunday attendance of about forty people, is the only Catholic church in the county.

Jean Bryant from St. Luke's met with townspeople from other churches and reported back to the parish. The small community prayed about a response and, despite the poverty of many of its own members, St. Luke's decided, in the words of parishioner Vonda Keon, to "take up our burden for the poor." Jean Bryant became one of the founders of the parish food pantry.

After learning about the Mississippi Food Network, which distributes dry products and nonperishable cans of vegetables, meat, and fruit to the poor through churches and other agencies, three parishioners from St. Luke's traveled more than two hours to the Network's headquarters in Jackson, Mississippi, for an orientation session. There they learned how to manage their inventory, how to order their products, and how to screen their clients. Persons requesting assistance have to fill out a client eligibility form which asks information regarding number of people in family; proof of income; proof of residence; and personal identification. Sometimes the rules do not apply, especially if someone has just lost their job, and so on. Food from the Network, which comes from government surplus and America's Second Harvest, costs churches like St. Luke's twelve cents a pound. Donations from a few parishioners provided the seed money to get the project started.

St. Luke's food pantry, called Our Daily Bread, takes place once a month on a Saturday. The week before, volunteers pick up the food in Grenada, a town about an hour's drive from Bruce. Other volunteers then bag the groceries. When Our Daily Bread began in the summer of 2000, it distributed food to thirty-five people in the first month. In a recent month, it gave away more than three hundred fifty bags of food.

The food pantry remains an ecumenical effort, which also depends on the generosity of local stores and civic organizations. Members of the Bruce African Methodist Episcopal Church donate funds; so do members of the Bruce United Methodist Church. They also help bag food, and their minister, Brother Rex Wilburn, regularly travels to Grenada with Scott Keon from St. Luke's to pick up the food. Members of the Baptist Women's Prayer Circle help, too. So do the local Piggly Wiggly, the Big Star grocery chain, the Bruce Furniture store, and the Rotary Club.

St. Luke's parishioners are proud of their work. St. Luke's is a mission church under the auspices of Glenmary Home Missioners and there is no resident priest. The parish administrator is now Sister Mary Jean Morris, OSF, but the parishioners opened Our Daily Bread in a period when they had no parish administrator. Sister Mary Jean says, "The people at St. Luke's have a deep spirituality. They are generous and caring because they have been close to poverty themselves."

How-To Guidelines

Here are six steps to opening a Food Pantry in your parish.

- Survey the unmet needs in your area. Are there any other food pantries currently operating? Who will you serve?

- Discuss your plans with the parish staff. Consult with diocesan ministries to understand the larger picture and to find out what resources they might offer you and what pitfalls you might encounter.

- Discuss the idea with other churches, religious groups, and civic organizations in the area. How can you work together? What resources and talents can they provide?

- Be very specific as you plan. Where will you operate? How often will you be open? Where will you obtain the food you distribute? How will you fund the necessary expenses of a food pantry?

- Once you have gathered information, schedule an organizational meeting open to all in the parish who are interested.

- Assign tasks with deadlines. Who will research sources of food? Who will contact social service agencies whose clients might need your services? Who will organize volunteers in the ongoing effort to pick up the food, bag it, and distribute it? Set a realistic opening date.

Reach Into the Collection Basket

Have you been searching for a way to involve more members of your parish in giving to the poor? Have you wanted to make more people-to-people connections? Here's a way to raise the awareness of every single person in the pews on the First Sunday of Advent.

On the First Sunday of Advent at Spirit of Christ Church in Arvada, Colorado, members of the community get to take something from the collection basket. Sounds a bit strange, doesn't it, when the purpose of this Reverse Collection is actually to give to the poor and needy in the surrounding areas?

What the parishioners take is a color-coded tag. Each tag contains details about someone who needs to be remembered this Christmas season—first name, age, and special request. The tags are color-coded to correspond to a particular organization. Blue tags might be keyed to a home for unwed mothers; yellow to a rehab center for young boys; green for a drug and alcohol transition program; white for a nearby nursing home. During November the parish solicits lists of names and requests from local organizations; volunteers then transfer the individual names to the appropriate tags.

Parishioners are asked to return the tags—with the wrapped gifts they have purchased—to the Community Center where parish volunteers have placed large posters in different spaces around the room. Each poster is decorated with a color-coded bow that matches the color of a tag. Parishioners then place their gift in the appropriate place. Representatives of the various organizations are expected to send trucks to pick up their gifts.

The Reverse Collection has been an outstanding success at Spirit of Christ Church. Parishioners at the early Masses are asked not to take too many tags so that there are enough tags for all seven Masses. Those who happened to miss the collection will ask the parish staff, "Where can I get my tag? I was away last weekend." If there are any leftover tags, people are encouraged to stop by the parish office during the week.

And as for the recipients, Christmas is really Christmas. A boy at the rehab center requested a blender for the house; he received one. A woman and her children who were transitioning from a homeless shelter asked for "towels and a bathroom rug in forest green." Her thank-you note said, "I only make $700 a month and could never afford to buy a bathroom rug. Thank you so much."

There are many other benefits. Parish volunteers for this project may be people who can't make a year-round commitment or attend evening meetings, but they can help out for a few weeks a year. Their intangible gifts of time and talent have been called forth. By sending a collection basket through the church at each Mass the parish also enables more people to participate, broadening the social justice ministry to include not just a few but many. Sharing time, talent, and treasure takes on a new dimension in Arvada where the Spirit of Christ is alive.

How-To Guidelines

Here are five steps you can take to implement a Reverse Collection in your parish.

- Discuss the idea with the parish team. Assess what your parish already does for the poor and needy at Christmastime. Decide on your goals. What limitations do you have?

- Solicit advice and input from local social service agencies. What are their needs? Would they welcome such an activity? Are they staffed to play their roles?

- Form a committee and assign tasks. You will need someone to act as liaison with the agencies you choose to work with. You will need people to write out the tags, make the posters, be there to collect the gifts, and you will need to involve the ushers who will distribute the tags. Be sure they understand the project and can answer questions they may receive.

- Alert the parish by announcing the project a week or two earlier in the bulletin.

- A Reverse Collection is similar to a Giving Tree, which also has been successful and made into a Christmas tradition at many parishes.

Create a Parish Garden

Rick Klehr, a farmer who helped create "The Left Field" at St. Joan of Arc Church in downtown Minneapolis, Minnesota, says, "By planting a garden right here on our parish grounds, we have tried to inspire our parishioners, the neighbors, and the kids to see the wonder of creation." Through this garden project, St. Joan of Arc Church brought people together—and produced a bountiful crop of vegetables, flowers, and herbs.

It seemed such an unlikely idea—a vegetable garden on the grounds of an inner city parish. But the Eco-Spirituality Ministry team at St. Joan of Arc was undeterred. They had several goals:

1. They wanted to help parishioners and neighbors understand that they could take some responsibility for food production and for wise use of urban land.

2. They wanted to bridge the gap between parishioners, many of whom commute to the church from the suburbs, and the neighbors, mostly African-American and Southeast Asian families who are not Catholics.

3. Finally, they hoped to involve the neighborhood children, who were accustomed to playing ball on the parish grounds, but had no familiarity with gardening.

The pastor, Father George Wertin, who had once preached in a homily, "Everyone should grow something, even if it's just in a little flower pot," became an enthusiastic supporter of "The Left Field," as the parish garden is called.

Work began in the spring of 2001 with "The Big Dig." Twenty-four people showed up on a Saturday in April to turn over the soil. Dan Chouinard, one of the organizers of the garden, says, "We introduced ourselves, said a prayer, and dug in." Two weeks later, the group planted the 20- by 30-foot garden and, throughout the summer, a core of ten people came twice a week, on Wednesday evenings and on Sundays, to till, weed, and care for the plants. Dan adds, "Each time we gathered, we would spread a blanket on the ground and have something to eat. The neighborhood kids started coming to see what we were doing." On Sundays, they served coffee in the garden and invited people to stop by and visit after Mass.

The team raised an impressive variety of vegetables, including several kinds of lettuce, beans, and tomatoes, plus spinach, broccoli, cabbage, pumpkins, turnips, cucumbers, onions, and herbs. They also planted a large zinnia patch and, during the summer, they frequently gave away the flowers as a way of saying, "Welcome to our garden."

The highlight of the gardeners' season was, of course, a bountiful harvest. As crops ripened, they sometimes gave produce away in the neighborhood. On the last Saturday in September, the parish sponsored a Farmer's Market, where the Eco-Spirituality Ministry team sold produce from "The Left Field," as well as vegetables parishioners had grown in their own home gardens. The event raised $1,250 for Second Harvest, the country's second-largest hunger-relief organization.

Rick Klehr, who along with Dan Chouinard organized "The Left Field," says, "We wanted to encourage people to become closer to the earth." Judging from the success of their first Farmer's Market, the Eco-Spirituality Ministry team at St. Joan of Arc has indeed succeeded in spreading their message.

How-To Guidelines

Here are five steps to creating your own Parish Garden.

- If you would like to create a garden, look at your parish grounds for an appropriate place. Is there an area that can be dedicated to such a use? Remember that you can start small. Discuss the idea with the pastoral team, the parish council, religious education teachers, and any other ministers you think might be interested.

- Visit the St. Joan of Arc Web site for photographs of their harvest and for a timeline of their gardening chores: www.stjoan.com/esfr.htm.

- Recruit some knowledgeable gardeners to help organize the garden: to select the appropriate crops, buy the seeds, and so on. Recruit volunteers to help throughout the gardening season. Provide supervision for the volunteers in what may be new chores for them; provide a spiritual context by opening each session with a prayer; provide hospitality with drinks and simple snacks.

- Involve the entire parish and surrounding community. Publish updates regularly in the parish bulletin or on simple flyers. Plan neighborhood/parish events, as appropriate. If your garden is large enough, follow the example of "The Left Field" and arrange a Farmer's Market. Have a mid-summer picnic or a Sunday ice-cream get-together for the children.

- If your parish does not have an Eco-Spirituality Ministry, and you would like to know more about such a ministry, here is what Tom Smith-Myott, Coordinator of Adult Formation at St. Joan of Arc, writes. He describes Eco-Spirituality as "the growing awareness that we need to consider the creation that supports and sustains us. When we talk about right relationships, we talk about not only our relationships with God, ourselves, and one another, we also talk about right relationships with creation around us, with the earth, and its creatures. We are challenged to change our behavior to act justly and wisely in our care for all of creation. An Eco-Spirituality Ministry in a parish draws attention to local issues and tries to educate, persuade, and effect change on environmental justice issues. Growing a garden is just one way (a very enjoyable way!) of focusing attention on the everyday goodness of God."

Resources

Here are just a few of many scriptural references you might want to use for prayer and reflection as you consider an Eco-Spirituality Ministry in your parish.

- Genesis, Chapter 1 and 2. The Creation story. "God saw everything that he had made, and indeed, it was very good" (1:31).

- Isaiah 65:18. "Be glad and rejoice forever in what I am creating."

- Psalm 104. A song of praise to God the Creator and Provider. "O LORD, how manifold are your works!" (verse 24).

- John 1:1–3. "All things came into being through him, and without him not one thing came into being" (verse 3).

Also be aware that the United States Conference of Catholic Bishops (USCCB) launched its Environmental Justice Program in 1993. The purpose of the USCCB program is "to help educate and motivate Catholics to a deeper respect for creation and to engage parishes in activities aimed at dealing with environmental problems, particularly as they affect the poor." For more complete information, including an overview of their programs, go to www.usccb.org/sdwp/ejp/index.htm.

～

Feed the Elderly Poor

"There are many kinds of hunger," says Cindy Broyer, who started the Dinner Bell at St. Elizabeth Ann Seton Church in Fryeburg, Maine. "We feed those who need food, those who need companionship, and those who need to serve others." Read about a rural soup kitchen with an extra dimension.

Ten years ago, when Cindy Broyer began the Dinner Bell program in her parish, St. Elizabeth Ann Seton Church in Fryeburg, Maine, there was one obvious goal: to feed the elderly poor. Parishioners very quickly discovered that some of the people who came were more lonely than hungry; they needed fellowship as well as food. And, in this small parish of four hundred families, there were others who said, "I have plenty of food and fellowship, but I have a hunger to do something for others." It is the hallmark of the Dinner Bell to attempt to feed all of these hungers.

The Dinner Bell rings in Fryeburg once a week, on Wednesday evenings, at 5 P.M. from September to June. Donations of food come from local storekeepers. Other supplies come from an ecumenical food bank and from a federal government program. Volunteers prepare the meals in the parish kitchen. On any given Wednesday, there might be twenty to twenty-two volunteers, cooking, serving at the buffet, and summoning people from the tables to the buffet line in an orderly fashion. The number of guests hovers around 150, rising to 175 during the holiday season. Most of the guests are the elderly poor. But, as Cindy Broyer points out, "These people are not necessarily starving. One woman said to me, 'I haven't had dessert in I don't know how long.'" All are welcome at the Dinner Bell.

How-To Guidelines

Here are five steps to starting a Dinner Bell program in your parish.

- Discuss the idea with the pastoral staff. Determine the needs of your parish community and the wider community where you live. Will you be duplicating services provided elsewhere?

- Talk to people in your diocesan offices and from other churches, synagogues, and mosques in your area. Consider a multi-parish or an interfaith effort. In rural Mississippi, for example, a tiny mission parish sparked just such an endeavor. (See page 59.)

- Consider your resources. Do you have a kitchen and appropriate facilities for cooking, serving, and storing food? How many guests can you accommodate? How will you finance the effort? Can you count on sufficient ongoing donations of money or food? Can you enlist enough volunteers?

- Schedule a planning meeting for all interested groups. Assign responsibilities for different tasks and create a time line with realistic deadlines for all to follow. Investigate all federal and local laws that apply to such endeavors; be sure you meet all requirements.

- Spread the word of your Dinner Bell among the social service agencies in your area. Do not open until you are sure you can commit to providing food on a regular, ongoing schedule.

∼

Create a Funeral Dinner Ministry

Marlys Sinnott remembers how her parish, St. Patrick Church, reached out to her family when her daughter-in-law died last year. "A lot of people who came to the funeral came from other states. They appreciated getting a good meal and getting to say good-bye to us. Dinner at the church made it like family." Read how this parish's Funeral Dinner Ministry works.

In the small town of Rolla, Missouri, Lora Killian has experienced St. Patrick's Funeral Dinner Ministry from both the receiving side and the giving side. "When I was fifty-three, my husband died unexpectedly. I had seven children, one still in high school and two in college. There were one hundred people at the funeral. I could never have hosted such a crowd." Now Lora serves as coordinator, a role she has played for ten years.

Her ministry begins as soon as she receives word of a funeral. She finds out all the details—date, time, and the number of people who might attend—and then gets on the phone to the telephone committee. These four people are responsible for asking others to provide food for the funeral dinner. By calling all parishioners in alphabetical order, the committee eventually involves everyone in this important ministry.

Parishioners send casseroles, salads, and desserts—enough for ten servings. Lori says they have never had anyone refuse; people who work buy salads at a deli or bagged salad and dressing in a supermarket. The parish supplies roast beef or ham, which someone on the team cooks at home. The parish also provides paper products, rolls, soft drinks, ice, tea, and coffee.

On the day of the funeral, a team of parishioners works in the kitchen. Depending on the number of guests at the dinner, the team can be as few as three or as many as five. They reheat casseroles, slice the meat, prepare and dress the salads, fix the coffee and tea. They set up the buffet table, serve, and clean up. A group of retired men from the parish helps to set up the tables and chairs in the parish hall.

Families cannot pay for this service, but they can make a donation to the church. The Funeral Dinner Ministry pays for the food and staples that the parish provides from its own funds, which in turn come from the parish budget or from separate donations.

The funeral dinner usually follows the burial service, but if the burial is held at a distant location, then the dinner is served immediately following the funeral Mass.

The Funeral Dinner Ministry has been an important part of St. Patrick's for more than twenty years. Pat Smith, a parishioner who currently serves on the team, says, "It's one of the most important things we do at church, a positive thing in a time of sorrow. It's a ministry we will all need at some time in our lives."

How-To Guidelines

Here are six steps for initiating a Funeral Dinner Ministry in your parish.

- Discuss the idea with the parish staff. What are their concerns? What modifications and adjustments will you want to make for your own community?

- Describe the proposed ministry in the parish bulletin. Solicit volunteers. Schedule a planning meeting for all who are interested in joining this ministry.

- From among the volunteers, select a coordinator. If you have a large parish with many funerals, perhaps two or more people could share the responsibilities.

- Organize the teams. Prepare careful job descriptions for each team so that everyone knows what needs to be done, by whom, and by when. Encourage the various teams to meet separately, if necessary, for further planning.

- After the first few dinners have taken place, schedule an assessment meeting. Ask what is working and what may need to be adjusted. You may want to invite some of the parishioners who were the recipients of the ministry to this meeting and ask for their responses.

- Keep careful records so those who continue the ministry will have guidelines to follow.

~

Become a Minister of Praise and Mercy

Encouraging the sick, the elderly, and homebound parishioners to serve in a ministry for the parish can seem a daunting task. Is it even possible? Here's a wonderful way to make it happen, a way that nourishes souls and offers real spiritual benefits to the parish.

Ten years ago, Dolores Kurzdorfer, from St. Leo's Parish in Buffalo, New York, was taking communion to the sick in her parish when she began to wonder how she could encourage them to be more involved in parish life. "These folks just seemed so isolated," she says.

A friend told her about Ministry of Praise and Mercy, a simple, easy-to-implement program started by Sister Mary Charla Gannon, RSM, in Chicago.

Ministry of Praise and Mercy focuses on prayer—something anyone can do anywhere, anytime. It doesn't require physical mobility or transportation or scheduling. "It is really an enhancement of the Morning Offering," Sister Mary Charla says. "We can help the sick or the elderly center their day on prayer and they can help us by speaking to God for us."

The program, as she designed it, gives dignity and identity and attention to the life of prayer in a parish. It also gives attention and respect to the sick. The pastor commissions the ministers at a special ceremony at church. He gives each a prayer book, a cross, and a certificate. Throughout the year the pastor and/or the Ministry of Praise and Mercy leaders send a monthly letter to the ministers requesting their prayers for particular intentions. Sometimes the petitions arise out of needs in the community; sometimes they come from liturgical seasons like Lent or Advent.

At St. Bede's Parish in Chicago, where Sister Mary Charla first instituted the program, the pastor initiated it by speaking from the altar, telling the entire parish, "This is the most important work in the parish. Prayer supports everything else we do."

The National Office of Ministry of Praise and Mercy, now run by the Franciscan Sisters of Our Lady of Grace, offers information packets, which contain a sample commissioning rite, the prayer book, and a certificate. Subsequent individual packets are available for each minister. The Ministry of Praise and Mercy has now reached into every state, and the materials are also available in Spanish. (See ordering information at end of this article.)

At St. Leo's, where there are now approximately seventy-five Ministers of Praise and Mercy, the program is an unqualified success. The pastor maintains personal contact with each minister. He sends birthday cards and he often receives thank-you notes for his monthly letters. Dolores Kurzdorfer receives requests for new prayer books when the original wears thin. Some families have framed the certificate for their elderly relatives and the ministers proudly display it in their living rooms. Obituaries have mentioned that the deceased was a Minister of Praise and Mercy, adding to the dignity of the ministry and of the individual—as well as enhancing the role of prayer in the life of the community.

How-To Guidelines

Here are six easy steps to starting a Ministry of Praise and Mercy in your parish.

- Speak with the pastor to be sure of his interest and support. Offer to send for an information packet ($12 plus postage and handling) that will answer any further questions. Ordering information is given at the end of this article.

- Discuss the Ministry of Praise and Mercy with parish ministers who visit the sick and homebound. Ask for reactions and comments.

- Decide on who will take responsibility for implementing—and continuing—the ministry.

- Decide on how the ministry will be announced and publicized in the parish. Will the pastor announce it from the pulpit? Will you announce it in the weekly bulletin?

- Think about how many ministers you are likely to attract. Set a time frame for inviting ministers to serve and for ordering individual kits. (These kits cost $10 each and contain the prayer book and the certificate.)

- Schedule a Commissioning Ceremony appropriate for your community. (The information packet contains a sample commissioning service.) You may want to do it during a Sunday liturgy. Think about transportation. Will you need volunteers for the occasion?

Here is ordering information for the Ministry of Praise and Mercy:

The Ministry of Praise and Mercy
Franciscan Sisters of Our Lady of Grace
5300 S. Natoma Avenue
Chicago, IL 60638

To order the information kit, which includes a sample certificate, a commissioning service, a prayer book, and helpful how-to-start assistance for parishes, send $12 plus $5.50 shipping and handling to the preceding address. Subsequent individual kits, to be distributed to each minister, include a certificate to be signed by the pastor and a prayer book. They are $10 each and are usually ordered in quantities of 25, 50, and 100. Smaller orders can be accommodated. An order form with shipping and handling costs is included with the information kit.

Allow at least three weeks for delivery.

Social Justice

Serve a Hunger Banquet

W*e live in affluence. We have no idea of what goes on in the Third World. The Hunger Banquet opens up our eyes." Kathy Early and her daughter Megan, a sophomore in college, were both changed by attending a Hunger Banquet at Holy Spirit Church in Virginia Beach, Virginia. Read how this parish organized a Lenten activity that effectively reaches all ages from high-school students to senior citizens.*

In Lent 2000, Holy Spirit Church organized its first Hunger Banquet, under the leadership of Robin Meyers, Coordinator of Social Ministry. About one hundred people attended, from high-school students to senior citizens.

As guests arrived, they were randomly given color-coded slips of paper that contained the name of the country they would represent. The ten people who represented the richest countries in the developed world were assigned to sit at an elegant table with linen tablecloth, china plates, silverware, glasses, and floral centerpiece. They were served by a waitress and were asked if they wanted seconds. Thirty people, representing less wealthy countries that were still in the developed world, were seated at tables with no tablecloth. They used paper plates and plastic utensils and were served one small serving of meat and one small serving of vegetable. Food was placed on the tables family style; if one guest took too much from the serving bowl, the others had to do without their share. The remaining sixty people, representing countries in the developing world, sat on the floor, and received a small bowl of rice and a paper cup of colored water. The water was colored with food dye to demonstrate the fact that people in the developing world don't even have clean drinking water. (Additional details from Catholic Relief Services, which created the format for hunger banquets, appear in the Resources section that follows.)

Megan Early served as a waitress at the table of plenty for the first Hunger Banquet. She remembers, "People at that table couldn't finish eating. No one took too much because they felt so uncomfortable. They were not allowed to give any food to the people on the floor because the purpose of the banquet is to demonstrate how it really is in the world."

To bring the message of the evening into focus, Robin Meyers arranged a short program while people were eating. It began with a prayer and an explanation of the evening and included two speakers. Patrice Schwermer, Social Justice Minister at St. Pius X Church in Norfolk, Virginia, spoke about her experiences in Chiapas, Mexico, and about national and global hunger. Parishioners John and Terry Gallegos talked about what they had observed in Haiti.

Patrice Schwermer says, "I tried to explain that there is enough food in the world to feed each person a daily diet of 2,300 calories. The issue is one of distribution. I think the Hunger Banquet really helps people understand what the global situation looks like and how we participate in it. Once people become aware, change begins."

Holy Spirit Church found that the people who attended were very moved by the experience and plans to continue serving Hunger Banquets.

How-To Guidelines

Here are five steps for serving a Hunger Banquet in your parish.

- Send for a copy of the *Operation Rice Bowl Community and Parish Guide,* "Pray, Fast, Learn, Give."

- Read the pages devoted to the Hunger Banquet and discuss the details with the pastoral team. Can your parish participate during the next Lenten season? Do you wish to co-sponsor with another parish? Plan ahead!

- Decide on when and where you will serve the Banquet. How many people can you accommodate? Think about who will attend. Do you want to attract teenagers? Young adults? All parishioners?

- At an organizational meeting, ask for volunteers to serve on committees that will handle all aspects of the event—publicity, food preparation and service, educational materials on hunger and poverty, program arrangements, including speakers and prayers, cleanup. Set time lines for all committee activities.

- Publicize the Hunger Banquet in the parish bulletin and, depending on the audience you have selected, in religious education classes, in confirmation classes, in local newspapers, in nearby schools and high schools, in other houses of worship.

Resources

Materials in the Lenten guide include not only instructions for the banquet, but also discussion and reflection questions, optional activities, suggested readings, and a World Awareness Quiz, which can be duplicated and distributed to the banquet guests.

- Hunger Banquet instructions are available, in English and Spanish, in the *Operation Rice Bowl Community and Parish Guide,* "Pray, Fast, Learn, Give," published by Catholic Relief Services. Available from Catholic Relief Services, 209 West Fayette Street, Baltimore, MD 21201-3443. Telephone: 410-625-2220. Online: www.catholicrelief.org.

$\sim$

Paint a Rainbow of Hope

Eileen Sammon remembers, "Seven of us went to see a film, and we came home changed. We had been called to do something about poverty, and we did. We started Rainbow of Hope." Learn about the film that motivated these women and about the outreach ministry they started at their parish, St. Ann's Church in Ossining, New York.

As part of an Ursuline Jubilee celebration, Sister Eileen Finnerty, an Ursuline nun and pastoral associate at St. Ann's Church, invited seven women from the parish to a lecture by Father James Hug, SJ, and the showing of a video, *A*

Contemporary Meditation on the Cross. The video uses a combination of black-and-white photography, blunt statistics, meditative music, and reflections on the Spirit to present a powerful motivational message about caring for the poor. (More information about the video appears in the Resources section that follows.) Seeing the video was "a graced moment" for the women, Eileen Sammon says. They came back to their parish knowing they wanted to get involved in caring for the poor.

They chose to create a Rainbow of Hope that assists St. Ann's Orphanage for Girls in Guyana, a mission of the Ursuline Sisters. Girls at the orphanage range in age from two to eighteen. The original seven women reached out to all of their parishioners by individual letters, by ongoing notices in the parish bulletin, by a display at the back of the church.

After Eileen Sammon spoke about Rainbow of Hope at Sunday Masses, several women volunteered to help. Betty Boyle makes tote bags that her daughter, a teacher, sells to friends and co-workers. In each bag, a note says, "For the benefit of the students in St. Ann's Orphanage in Guyana." Mary Lanni writes birthday cards to the girls in the orphanage; Joanna DiDomenico organizes the letters to go out to parishioners, asking for their financial support.

In its first year, Rainbow of Hope raised more than $9,000 for the Orphanage. The effort has helped send two girls from the Orphanage on to higher education. This year, the women say, they are on target to raise a good deal more money.

As important as the money, however, is the ongoing contact between the children in Guyana and the parishioners in Ossining. As part of the display at the back of the church, Rainbow of Hope keeps an "open book" that contains lists of the needs of the orphanage, thank-you notes from the children, photographs, and an accounting of all funds raised and how they were spent. The original seven women who started Rainbow of Hope, together with their newer volunteers and the other St. Ann's parishioners who participate, believe they are doing what they have been called to do—care for the poor. Joanna DiDomenico says, "This activity brings us closer to God."

How-To Guidelines

Here are five steps for encouraging members of your parish to reach out to the poor.

- Assess the outreach programs that are alive and well in your parish. How many parishioners are motivated to care for the poor? What encouragement, guidance, and assistance does the pastoral team provide? What more could the parish be doing?

- Consider your own resources. Do you have any contacts—through parishioners, the diocese, or local religious communities—with towns or projects or institutions that need your assistance? Personal connections can encourage more people to get involved. In Ossining, for example, pastoral associate Sister Eileen Finnerty provided the connecting link to the orphanage in Guyana.

- Decide on an organizational plan for your effort. Will it be the responsibility of an Outreach Ministry already operating in the parish? Or will this become a separate team effort? Be sure you have solid, enthusiastic leadership in place before you proceed.

- Plan a campaign that will motivate parishioners to become involved. Share information resources with potential volunteers.

- Develop goals for the project. Recruit necessary volunteers. Spread the word. Ask for prayers in support of the endeavor. Persevere.

Resources

Any of the following resources might provide an impetus for change or a raised consciousness among parishioners.

- *A Contemporary Meditation on the Cross.* In a 26-minute video, Father James Hug, SJ, presents a visual meditation on the cross with photo images, statistics, music, and prayerful reflections. How is Christ crucified in the contemporary global community with growing gaps between rich and poor? The video helps us discern how we are to stand at the foot of the cross today. Ordering information: Center of Concern, 1225 Otis St. NE, Washington, DC 20017; 202-635-2757, ext. 111; or online at www.coc.org.

- The United States Catholic Bishops, "Economic Justice for All: A Pastoral Letter on Catholic Social Teaching and the U.S. Economy," 1986. The economy must be measured by how it protects the dignity of every person. Each of us must ask: What does the economy do to people? What does the economy do for people? Available from the United States Conference of Catholic Bishops by calling 1-800-235-8722; or online at www.usccb.org/publishing/socialjustice.htm#economicjustice.

- The four great social justice encyclicals of the Roman Catholic Church. Each offers wonderful teachings on individual human dignity, the value of work, and the imperative of providing the means for all to feed, clothe, and shelter themselves.

  1. Pope Leo XIII, "Rerum Novarum," 1891. Available online at www.vatican.va/holy_father/leo_xiii/encyclicals/documents/hf _l-xiii_enc_15051891_rerum-novarum_en.html.

  2. Pope Pius XI, "Quadregesimo Anno," 1941, delivered on the fortieth anniversary of "Rerum Novarum." Available at www.vatican.va /holy_father/pius_xi/encyclicals/documentshf_pxi_enc _19310515_quadragesimo-anno_en.html.

  3. Pope John Paul II, "Laborem Exercens," 1981, delivered on the ninetieth anniversary of "Rerum Novarum." Available online at www.vatican.va /holy_father/john_paul_ii/encyclicals/documents/hf_jp-ii _enc_14091981_laborem-exercens_en.html.

  4. Pope John Paul II, "Centesimus Annus," 1991, delivered on the one-hundredth anniversary of "Rerum Novarum." Available online at www.vatican.va/holy_father/john_paul_ii/encyclicals/documents /hf_jp-ii_enc_01051991_centesimus-annus_en.html.

Make a Big Difference in a Simple Way

"Actions speak louder than words. What we do in our daily lives does make a difference." Wanda Lickteig, a member of St. Ignatius Church in San Francisco, took her own words to heart and helped educate her community on the economic justice implications of buying coffee. This parish is making a difference in the lives of poor farmers.

At St. Ignatius Church, several parishioners, who were already active in Social Justice Ministry, began to ask themselves what their community could do about global economic issues. How, in very specific ways, could they show their concern for the poor in developing nations? The parish, they believed, would be acting out of its Christian commitment. Wanda Lickteig says, "Being involved in social justice issues is what the gospel asks us to do."

After much study and discussion, St. Ignatius Church chose to advocate and promote fair trade coffee as their commitment to economic justice. Fair trade coffee is coffee that is independently certified to be grown by worker-owned and democratically-run cooperatives; harvested by workers who earn a living wage; free of child labor; and cultivated with environmentally sustainable methods. (More information about fair trade coffee appears in the Resources section that follows.)

Members of the Social Justice Ministry committed to serving only fair trade coffee in their homes and at parish coffee hours, even though the coffee costs slightly more than regular coffee. The parish bookstore started to sell fair trade coffee. The group distributed flyers listing the stores and cafés in the San Francisco area where fair trade coffee was sold. They ran educational programs after Sunday Masses and explained the campaign in the parish bulletin.

St. Ignatius joined with two other Catholic churches in San Francisco in this effort. Together the three parishes comprise nearly five thousand families and by encouraging all the members of their communities to request fair trade coffee in stores and local coffee shops and restaurants, they were able to make a difference. A letter signed by all three pastors was mailed to owners of stores and cafés in the neighborhood, inviting their participation in the effort and promising to list their name on a flyer distributed to all five thousand parish households.

The issue galvanized members of the Social Justice Ministry and their enthusiasm affected others in the parish and surrounding neighborhoods. Julia Dowd, pastoral associate at St. Ignatius, sums up the endeavor: "We saw that we could have an impact and influence others through a simple cup of coffee."

Parishioners at St. Ignatius chose fair trade coffee as the area where they would make evident their commitment to faith and justice. You may want to follow your commitment to Gospel values in some other way.

How-To Guidelines

Here are seven steps to selecting and pursuing an economic justice issue for your parish.

- Read "Economic Justice for All: Pastoral Letter on Catholic Social Teaching and the U.S. Economy," written by the U.S. Catholic Bishops. (Washington, DC: National Conference of Catholic Bishops, 1986.) You can order copies for your parish library by calling the USCCB Printing Office at 1-800-235-8722 or by going online to www.usccb.org/publishing/socialjustice.htm.

- Schedule small group discussions for the pastoral team, the Social Justice Ministry team, and other interested parishioners. (You will find excellent resource materials for these discussions in the IMPACT series available from RENEW International. To see those titles dealing particularly with social and ecological issues, go to www.renewintl.org/Resources/Pages/faithshare.html.)

- Investigate issues that might affect or interest your particular community; investigate the organizations involved in the issue. Contact the Social Justice Ministry in your diocese to find out what is already going on in your area. Also, seek help from them to get the resources you need for your efforts.

- Create a plan of action. How will you make a difference? Be specific. Be sure your ideas are practical and that they can be executed by the gifts and resources available within your community. Also consider joining with other parishes or with a national effort.

- Present the economic justice issue to the parish. Ask for their support. Be prepared to educate, to persuade, and to lead. Have written materials available; invite speakers; encourage discussion and faith-sharing groups or small Christian communities. Solicit volunteers, especially from among young adults and teens.

- Stay committed. Stay enthusiastic. Enlist the prayers of the entire community, especially those who cannot be actively involved.

- When you are ready, take your endeavor to the wider community. Contact newspapers and other media outlets. Plan events. Reach out to the schools. Remember that by your actions, you are spreading the Gospel message.

Resources

These two Web sites offer information about fair trade coffee:

- TransFair USA is a non-profit organization that certifies and promotes fair trade coffee: www.transfairusa.org.

- Global Exchange is a non-profit research, education, and action center that promotes environmental, political, and social justice around the world: www.globalexchange.org/ economy/coffee/.

~

Build Gospel Bridges

"It was an awesome and uncomfortable experience that I would recommend to everyone." That's how Madge McCready describes the week she and her husband, Tom, spent building a house for a poor family in Juarez, Mexico. Their parish community, Spirit of Christ Church in Arvada, Colorado, invites its members to experience firsthand the meaning of Christ's social teaching.

"It's all about building bridges," says Deacon Mike Howard when he explains his parish community's mission experience, which is called Southern Exposure. Three bridges, a barbed-wire fence, and a dried-up creek separate Ciudad Juarez, Mexico, and El Paso, Texas. Southern Exposure, which offers immersion programs and build-a-house construction assistance, reaches across cultural as well as physical barriers. It invites American participants to understand more deeply the reality of Mexican lives and to experience in their own lives the meaning of the Gospel message.

By any measure the program is a success. Since March 2000, under the guidance of Deacon Mike, Pat Vachon (another parishioner from Spirit of Christ Church), and Rev. Stan Martinka (an American priest working as a missionary in Juarez), volunteers have constructed more than forty houses. The houses are simple—20 foot by 20 foot cinder-block buildings with one wood partition—but they are enough to protect families who otherwise would have no shelter from wind and rain and cold.

Volunteers are organized into crews of ten to twelve people. Each crew spends a week in Juarez, usually completing one house, and each is responsible for raising the $2,600 it costs to build a house.

Volunteers pay their own transportation and a stipend of $100 a week for room and board. Southern Exposure provides a trained crew leader, accommodations at Casa de Esperanta (their own air-conditioned retreat house in Juarez), and transportation from El Paso.

Construction volunteers are required to attend two meetings before they leave for Juarez. At those meetings, team leaders explain what to expect and answer questions. Two weeks after each crew returns, there is a potluck dinner to celebrate and reflect on the experience.

Southern Exposure actually began ten years ago as a cultural immersion program. Deacon Mike and Father Stan worked together to bring Americans, mostly parishioners from Spirit of Christ Church, to Juarez to experience the Mexican culture. Participants toured schools, markets, and clinics and learned about the challenges of everyday life in Juarez. Now the immersion program and the construction projects exist side-by-side.

And participation is no longer limited to parishioners from Spirit of Christ Church. Through the Internet, Southern Exposure has spread its mission beyond Colorado and begun to organize volunteer crews from other states.

Ninety percent of the volunteers who go to Juarez want to return. But numbers alone cannot measure the success of the program. Deacon Mike and other participants agree; they have all brought back from Juarez far more than they gave during their time there. The experience changed their lives.

How-To Guidelines

Here are five ways your parish can initiate its own or join another parish's Mission Experience.

- Discuss the idea with the pastoral team, the Social Justice Ministry, outreach ministries in the parish and small Christian community members.

- Schedule small group discussions, open to all parishioners, of "The Church in America (Ecclesia in America)," the post-synodal Apostolic Exhortation issued by Pope John Paul II in 1999. (Sample excerpts and the Web site for the entire papal document appear in the Resources section that follows.)

- Investigate thoroughly the options open to your particular parish community. Do you want to initiate your own program? Do you have the organizational skills to do so? Would you prefer to join an already established effort, such as Southern Exposure, or Habitat for Humanity, or Catholic Relief Services, or one operating in your state? Do you want to initiate an international project or would you prefer to serve the poor in an area closer to home? There are, for example, many inner-city projects that make buildings habitable for families.

- Enlist the assistance of your diocesan offices. What already exists? Where is the greatest need? You could also discuss your idea with other parishes in your diocese. Consider starting (or joining) an ecumenical or interfaith effort.

- Once you have an idea of what your parish can do, build support for the effort within the community. Ask for prayers. Schedule meetings to explain to the parishioners what a Mission Experience would entail; invite speakers who have participated in such an effort. Reach out to teens and young adults. Enlist the support of the small Christian communities.

Resources

1. Here are three excerpts from "The Church in America (Ecclesia in America)," Pope John Paul II's post-synodal Apostolic Exhortation, issued in Mexico City on January 22, 1999, following the Special Assembly for America of the Synod of Bishops, held in the Vatican from November 16 to December 12, 1997. Consider using the text for small-group discussions and to motivate your parish to get involved in a Mission Experience.

- From section 52: "'Truly, I say to you, as you did it to one of the least of these my brethren, you did it to me' (Matthew 25:40; see 25:45). The awareness of communion with Christ and with our brothers and sisters, for its part the fruit of conversion, leads to the service of our neighbors in all their needs, material and spiritual, since the face of Christ shines forth in every human being."

- From section 58: "Concern for those most in need springs from a decision to love the poor in a special manner. This is a love which is not exclusive and thus cannot be interpreted as a sign of partiality or sectarianism; in loving the poor the Christian imitates the attitude of the Lord, who during his earthly life devoted himself with special compassion to all those in spiritual and material need.

  "The Church's work on behalf of the poor in every part of America is important; yet efforts are still needed to make this line of pastoral activity increasingly directed to an encounter with Christ who, though rich, made himself poor for our sakes, that he might enrich us by his poverty (see 2 Corinthians 8:9). There is a need to intensify and broaden what is already being done in this area, with the goal of reaching as many of the poor as possible. Sacred Scripture reminds us that God hears the cry of the poor (see Ps 34:7) and the Church must heed the cry of those most in need. Hearing their voice, 'she must live with the poor and share their distress. By her lifestyle, her priorities, her words and her actions, she must testify that she is in communion and solidarity with them.'"

- From section 64: "Since all people, whatever their race or condition, have been created by God in his image, it is necessary to encourage concrete programs, in which common prayer must play a part, aimed at promoting understanding and reconciliation between different peoples. These can build bridges of Christian love, peace, and justice between all men and women."

The entire text can be read at www.vatican.va/ holy_father/john_paul_ii /apost_exhortations/documents/hf_jp-ii_exh_22011999_ecclesia-in-america_en.html.

2. This Web site will give you more details about Southern Exposure, a Parish Mission Experience, encompassing both immersion and construction programs, established and run by members of Spirit of Christ Church in Arvada, Colorado: www.spiritofchrist.org/.

~

Ring Out the Death Penalty

"Tolling the bells is profound. It's a way to prayerfully and respectfully keep in our consciousness that every single person is made in God's image." Libbey Smith of Church of the Epiphany in Louisville, Kentucky, brought a national campaign of witness against the death penalty to her parish.

Many people have heard the words of the poem:

> *...any man's death diminishes me,*
> *because I am involved in Mankinde;*
> *And therefore never send to*
> *know for whom the bell tolls;*
> *It tolls for thee.*
>
> JOHN DONNE, "FOR WHOM THE BELL TOLLS"

But it took the insight of Sister Dorothy Briggs, a Dominican from Massachusetts, to use the familiar words to form a national campaign that offers churches, monasteries, abbeys, and other religious communities a prayerful yet public way to express their opposition to the death penalty.

Sister Dorothy credits Cardinal Jaime Sin of the Philippines with initiating the effort when he asked Catholic churches in his country to toll their bells to mourn the execution of a citizen there. Bishop Walter Sullivan of Richmond, Virginia, learned of the practice and wrote to all the churches in his diocese asking that those with bell towers toll their bells "on the evening of every execution until we bring an end to this inhumane practice."

For Whom the Bells Toll (FWBT) began as a national campaign in September 2000, and has already spread to churches and religious institutions in more than thirty-five states.

Libbey Smith from Church of the Epiphany in Louisville, Kentucky, came across information about the campaign on the Internet. (See the Resources section that follows for Web sites.) She investigated the project, presented it to her parish, and Epiphany has now incorporated For Whom the Bells Toll into the ministry of its Respect Life Committee.

Archbishop Thomas C. Kelly of Louisville is a supporter of the campaign. "If a parish has bells, they offer a good opportunity to speak in a reverential, non-confrontational way our Church's conviction about the sacredness of human life." The archbishop adds, "The bell campaign serves to remind everyone of the paramount value of compassion."

At Epiphany, the Respect Life Committee asked for volunteers who would be willing to ring the bells at 6 P.M. on the day of an execution. "We ring the bells for two minutes, as the national campaign suggests," Libbey explains. "We publish it in the bulletin so people will know why the bells are tolling. We have a brief prayer service at church and we not only name the person to be executed, but also the victims." (Epiphany's prayer service appears at the end of this article.) Sister Dorothy says the campaign has grown so fast that it seems to be taking on a life of its own. FWBT will continue until there is a moratorium on the death penalty or until the death penalty is abolished in this country. The project offers free brochures to those who want to help publicize FWBT and also offers suggestions for places of worship that don't have a bell but still want to participate in the campaign. Recently, Sister Dorothy began focusing her attention on all the Church-sponsored colleges and universities that have made public statements in opposition to the death penalty. "I think students are our natural allies and that they may be very instrumental in having the college or university administration publicly demonstrate by tolling the bells."

How-To Guidelines

Here are several steps to follow to initiate For Whom the Bells Toll in your parish.

- Research the origin, the aims, and the activities of For Whom the Bells Toll online at www.curenational.org/~bells/origin.html.

- Discuss the campaign with the pastoral staff and other ministries within the parish. Be sure to include teens and young adults in your discussions. If you sense a need for more education on the topic, you can do the following:

  1. Bring in a speaker to talk to parishioners about capital punishment. Your diocesan offices may be able to help you find the right person.

  2. Order informational materials for the parish. (A list appears in the Resources section that follows.) Make them available in the lobby or parish hall or greeting space. Mention them in the bulletin and, when appropriate, in homilies.

  3. Schedule small-group discussions. Make use of existing structures in your community, for example, religious education groups or small Christian communities.

- To plan your prayer services, you will need to know the dates of scheduled executions in the United States. The following Web site is one place to obtain such information: www.amnestyusa.org/abolish/pendex.html.

- When you believe the parish is ready to support For Whom the Bells Toll, describe the effort in your bulletin and ask for help from volunteers to ring the bells.

- If your parish does not have bells, investigate other ways of participating, such as hanging a banner, tying black ribbons on poles, or hanging a black drape outside the door of the church on the day of an execution.

- Publicize your efforts in the local media. Be prepared with flyers and brochures that describe the campaign in greater detail.

Sample Prayer Service

Church of the Epiphany uses this format for its brief prayer service whenever they toll the bells on the day of an execution. They adapt the prayer as necessary to reflect the identity and gender of the murderer and the victims.

"We gather together to mourn the execution of [fill in name]. *We ask that you support his family as they mourn his death."*

Have someone read Psalm 23.

"We also offer our prayers for his victim, [fill in name]. *Please wrap your arms around his family and send them the support and comfort they need. Although the murder of their loved one was many years ago, they may need Your love more than ever now. We now ring this bell as a reminder that all life is sacred."*

Resources

Here are sources for more information on capital punishment.

- *Quest for Justice: A Compendium of Statements of the United States Catholic Bishops on the Political and Social Order 1966–1980,* edited by J. Brian Benestad and Francis J. Butler. Washington, D.C.: United States Catholic Conference, 1981. The U.S. Catholic Bishops speak out against the death penalty. Available through libraries.

- Pope John Paul II, "Evangelium Vitae," 1995. In 1995, Pope John Paul II wrote that in contemporary states where the option to remove the offender from further harm to society exists, cases where the death penalty should be used "are rare, if not practically nonexistent" (56). In 1997, the Vatican promulgated modifications to the language regarding capital punishment in the *Catechism of the Catholic Church.* The changes in paragraphs 2265, 2266, and 2267 were intended to reflect the same view expressed by Pope John Paul II. "*Evangelium Vitae*" is available at www.vatican.va/holy_father/john_paul_ii/ encyclicals/documents /hf_jp-ii_enc_25031995_evangelium-vitae_en.html.

- *Dead Man Walking.* Helen Prejean. (New York: Vintage Books/Random House, 1993.) Presents a compelling exploration of the death penalty. A Roman Catholic nun became the spiritual advisor to a condemned murderer who was soon executed. Powerfully and persuasively presented, with a compassion that embraces not only the terrified killer but the families of his victims. Catholic social teaching and Jesus' example serve as the lenses for reflection. Available through libraries or booksellers.

- *Reflections on Dead Man Walking.* Helen Prejean and Lucille Sarrat. Plainfield, N.J.: RENEW International (IMPACT Faith-Sharing Series), 2000. Materials for six weekly small community faith-sharing sessions based on the book above by Sr. Helen Prejean. Can be ordered by calling 1-888-433-3221 or online at www.renewintl.org/Resources/Pages/reflecimp.html.

- United States Catholic Conference of Bishops, "Statement on Capital Punishment." November 27, 1980. Can be ordered by calling 1-800-235-8722 or online at www.usccb.org/sdwp/national/criminal/death/deecu.htm.

- United States Catholic Conference of Bishops, "A Good Friday Appeal to End the Death Penalty," April 2, 1999. Can be ordered in English or Spanish by calling 1-800-235-8722 or online at www.usccb.org/sdwp/national /criminal/appeal.htm.

~

Care for the Stranger Among Us

"My grandfather was an immigrant laborer, a blacksmith. Now these parishioners need our help. It's our obligation to reach out to them." Dave Loritans is one of the founders of the Hispanic Employment Labor Project at St. Ann's Church in Ossining, New York. Read how this parish is reaching out to Hispanic immigrants in a variety of innovative ways.

A few years ago several young Hispanic parishioners went to visit Father Edward Byrne, pastor of St. Ann's Church, a multi-ethnic parish. They had been cheated of their wages, robbed of their jackets, and left miles from their homes. Searching for legal and economic solutions, Father Ed gathered a committee of parishioners, businessmen, and representatives from other churches in the area. How could they help retrieve the lost wages, which many other day workers were also reporting, without risking the safety of the men since so many of the immigrants were undocumented? (In the Resources section that follows, read about recent teachings of the Catholic Church on ministering to immigrants.)

Dave Loritans, one of the earliest members of the committee, remembers that from the beginning the group saw itself as a church organization. "We wanted to make the process as amicable as possible. We wanted to try to engage the employers in dialogue and help them see their obligation to these workers."

The Hispanic Employment Labor Project (HELP) had begun. The group set up procedures that would meet those guidelines. First, someone makes a phone call to the employer on behalf of the workers. Then, the committee sends a friendly letter, followed by a second letter, if necessary, that states the workers' rights and mentions legal options, such as taking the employer to Small Claims Court. If none of the early steps are successful, a Spanish-speaking member of the committee will go to Small Claims Court with the immigrant.

The HELP committee meets once a month in the rectory at St. Ann's and reviews cases that are going to Small Claims Court. Volunteers who go to court with the immigrants are not lawyers, but are fluent in Spanish so they can communicate with the employee.

In addition to legal assistance, HELP runs ESL (English as a Second Language) classes for thirty to forty students. In these classes the teachers work with everyday words the students can use in their daily lives, both personal and on the job. They teach simple sentences and vocabulary the students will need—words like *cement, sand, tools, hammer,* and *saw.* The ESL teachers also help the immigrants document their labor. The men learn to note the license plate number of the truck that picks them up for work; they learn to write down the work they do, the number of hours they work, and where they work.

Another part of HELP (which, the committee notes, can also mean Help Educate Latino People) is a series of educational programs that takes place after the Hispanic Mass on Saturday night. The series covers health topics, such as tuberculosis and Lyme disease, immigration issues, housing issues, and financial advice. The immigrants, for example, are advised to get an IRS tax identification card and pay their taxes; to open a bank account; to begin to participate in the American economy, even if they don't have legal status.

Under the leadership of parishioner Eileen Sammon, HELP also contacted public agencies and social service organizations in the Ossining area to determine if they would assist the immigrants and if they had Spanish-speaking staff or volunteers. The committee then published a list, in Spanish, of those places that could offer assistance to Hispanic immigrants and distributed it to parishioners as well as others in the community. Among the places on the list are libraries; schools; a volunteer ambulance corps; Loaves and Fishes, a food distribution center; Birthright, which assists expectant mothers; Open Door, a medical facility; and the Ossining Senior Center.

HELP committee members know their pastoral services are desperately needed—and welcomed—by the immigrant community in their midst. If they needed evidence, they can look to a letter from two of the immigrants who, with the assistance of HELP, were able to retrieve lost wages. Enclosed with their thank-you note was a significant donation to HELP to continue the work.

How-To Guidelines

Here are seven steps to setting up a ministry for immigrants in your midst.

- Assess the situation in your community. Do you already reach out to welcome immigrants to liturgy and other church events? What are the needs of your immigrant parishioners? What needs are not being met? Take your time with this step. Consult with many people—immigrants, other parishioners, social service agencies, diocesan ministries, RENEW International.

- Assess the talents available to your parish community. Who has the necessary language skills? Who has counseling credentials? Legal skills? Immigration or housing expertise? Where will you find ministers with such skills? A successful ministry will meet the needs of the community with appropriate and necessary talents.

- Familiarize yourself, the pastoral team, and anyone who wants to become involved in this ministry with the recent teachings of the Catholic Church on immigration (see below for a brief summary of those teachings). Order educational materials from the U.S. Conference of Catholic Bishops and download information from Vatican Web sites. (A list of resources follows this article.) Schedule parish discussion groups; invite the small Christian communities in the parish to consider the topic; suggest "Welcoming the Stranger Among Us" as a topic for adult faith-formation classes.

• Form a core team to draft goals and objectives. What exactly will you do? Be specific. What assistance or guidance will you provide? By whom? And for whom? Set up time lines for completion of early organizational tasks. The need may be great, but don't be afraid to start small.

• As you proceed, develop coalitions with town officials, diocesan ministries, healthcare professionals, other local churches and places of worship, and so on.

• Recruit volunteers with the necessary skills. Ask for prayers and support from all parishioners.

• Study some recent teachings of the Catholic Church on immigrants.

1. Pope John Paul II has addressed the plight of immigrants in several papal documents. Here are a few excerpts to consider.

From the Message for World Migration Day 2000

"In many regions of the world today people live in tragic situations of instability and uncertainty. It does not come as a surprise that in such contexts the poor and the destitute make plans to escape, to seek a new land that can offer them bread, dignity, and peace.

"This is the migration of the desperate: men and women, often young, who have no alternative than to leave their own country to venture into the unknown. Every day, thousands of people take even critical risks in their attempts to escape from a life with no future. Unfortunately, the reality they find in host nations is frequently a source of further disappointment.

"At the same time, states with a relative abundance tend to tighten their borders under pressure from a public opinion disturbed by the inconveniences that accompany the phenomenon of immigration. Society finds itself having to deal with the 'clandestine,' men and women in illegal situations, without any rights in a country that refuses to welcome them, victims of organized crime or of unscrupulous entrepreneurs.... (4)

"The Church hears the suffering cry of all who are uprooted from their own land, of families forcefully separated, of those who, in the rapid changes of our day, are unable to find a stable home anywhere. She senses the anguish of those without rights, without any security, at the mercy of every kind of exploitation, and she supports them in their unhappiness." (6)

From the Post-Synodal Exhortation, "The Church in America"

"In its history, America has experienced many immigrations, as waves of men and women came to its various regions in the hope of a better future. The phenomenon continues even today, especially with many people and families from Latin American countries who have moved to the northern parts of the continent, to the point where in some cases they constitute a substantial part of the population. They often bring with them a cultural and religious heritage, which is rich in Christian elements. The Church is well aware of the problems created by this situation and is committed to spare no effort in developing her own pastoral strategy among these immigrant people, in order to help them settle in their new land and to foster a welcoming attitude among the local population, in the belief that a mutual openness will bring enrichment to all.

"Church communities will not fail to see in this phenomenon a specific call to live an evangelical fraternity and at the same time a summons to strengthen their own religious spirit with a view to a more penetrating evangelization." (65)

2. The U.S. Conference of Catholic Bishops issued a statement, "Welcoming the Stranger Among Us: Unity in Diversity" in November 2000. In the statement, the bishops first discuss the situation of immigrants in the United States and assert that the Church can offer pastoral care and social services to all people without condoning the actions of those who are undocumented immigrants. They state that while they recognize the government of the United States has the right to set immigration policies,

they affirm the human dignity of all, no matter what their legal status. The bishops then discuss the importance of welcoming newcomers and caring for their needs. After a discussion of some of the obstacles to a proper welcome—issues such as competition for resources and cultural fear—the bishops call on all Catholics to try to understand the strangers among them, to communicate with them, worship with them, minister to them. The bishops envision response at the national level, the diocesan level, and the parish level and they make some concrete suggestions. They conclude with a call to the "new evangelization" envisioned by Pope John Paul II in "The Church in America."

Resources

Here are some social justice documents on immigration.

- The text of the Message of the Holy Father for the World Migration Day 2000 is available at www.vatican.va/ holy_father/john_paul_ii/messages /migration/documents/hf_jp-ii_mes_21111999_world-migration-day -2000_en.html.

- The text of "The Church in America (Ecclesia in America)," a Post-Synodal Apostolic Exhortation issued by Pope John Paul II, in January 1999, is available at www.vatican.va/holy_father/john_paul_ii/apost_exhortations /documents/hf_jp-ii_exh_22011999_ecclesia-in-america_en.html.

- "Welcoming the Stranger Among Us," a statement of the U.S. Conference of Catholic Bishops (USCCB), issued on November 15, 2000, is available at www.usccb.org/mrs/unity.htm. You can also order from the USCCB a kit, "Welcoming the Stranger Among Us," which includes the U.S. Catholic Bishops' statement plus other resources, such as liturgy guides for parish teams, homily suggestions, religious education ideas, and a bibliography. To order: 1-800-235-8722, or online at www.usccb.org/mrs/parkit-eng.htm.

Spirituality

~

Encourage Multicultural
Devotion to Mary

Y*ou understand that Mary loves all of us, no matter what country we come from." Ottilie Sorrentino, a parishioner at St. Mary's Church, delights in all the different representations of Mary that people bring to the Crowning of Mary ceremony at her parish. Read about the way the parishioners have created a multicultural devotion to Mary.*

On the grounds of a busy suburban parish, St. Mary's Church, Colts Neck, New Jersey, the Grotto of Lourdes is a tranquil place, nestled against a hillside, near the St. Francis Meditation Garden. Throughout the year, the grotto is a spot for quiet prayer and meditation, but on the first Sunday of May each year the grotto is a colorful sight—filled with flowers, banners, and statues as parishioners gather for the annual Crowning of Mary.

The distinctive characteristic of this May Crowning is its multicultural dimension. As parishioners process from the church to the grotto, they carry banners and pictures of Mary as she has appeared in many different countries. The banners might include, for example, Our Lady of Czestochowa (Poland), Our Lady of Fátima (Portugal), Our Lady of Guadalupe (Mexico), Our Lady of Knock (Ireland), Our Lady of Lourdes (France). Parishioners decorate the banners with silk flowers or holy cards or photographs. (A Web site address which may be helpful appears in the Resources section that follows.)

The ceremony begins in the church after the noon Mass. After a traditional Marian hymn, the pastor, Father Edward Griswold, gives a homily, speaking about how Mary is revered around the world in many languages and cultures. He blesses the crown of silk flowers, which is then carried in procession to the grotto. Parishioners say the rosary during the procession. While Father Ed places the crown on Mary's head, the group sings the familiar "Mary, We Crown Thee."

The ceremony, which was created by the former pastor, Father Bill Bausch, is a longtime favorite of many parishioners. The festivities end in the parish hall with coffee and cake.

How-To Guidelines

Here are five steps to arranging a multicultural ceremony for a Crowning of Mary in your parish.

- Discuss the idea with the pastoral staff. What Marian events does your parish already schedule in May?

- Determine the level of interest in such an event. Will you need to do some instruction first to build an awareness of Mary's proper role in our salvation history? Will you want to include children and teenagers in the parish school and/or religious education program in the preparation and celebration?

- What cultural backgrounds are present in your community? How will you make all groups feel welcome and represented? Do some research on the various appearances of Mary and make background information available to all who are interested in helping prepare the event. (See Resources section that follows.) What special gifts can you draw forth from parishioners in art or music?

- Plan carefully; work with the Liturgy Committee to be sure the event is not only festive but also prayerful. Consider timing, location, prayers, music, and hospitality. For refreshments, think about ethnic cakes or other specialties, depending on the cultures within your community.

- Schedule a planning meeting and assign various tasks. Publicize the event in the bulletin and through the parish school and/or religious education program.

Resources

For more information about many different titles and representations of Mary, start with the excellent Marian Pages at www.udayton.edu/mary/.

~

Turn Everything Over to God

"Taizé prayer is like a sacred pause. I can bring everything in my life to this prayer service and turn it all over to God." Parishioner Vicki Tufano is just one of the hundreds of people who attend this once-a-month ecumenical prayer service at Ascension Church in Oak Park, Illinois.

On the first Friday of the month, at 7:30 P.M., hundreds of people of many faiths arrive at Ascension Church. They enter in silence. A greeter offers them a candle and a guide to the service. For the next hour, they will join together in a Taizé prayer service that includes song, silence, and Scripture.

Taizé (teh-ZAY) prayer began during World War II in France among an ecumenical community of monks who still live and pray together. Visitors from all over the world, especially young people, have prayed with the monks at Taizé. Its distinctive form of repetitive, meditative singing, interspersed with periods of silence, has spread far and wide. (More information about the Taizé community appears in the Resources section that follows.)

At Ascension, where David Anderson, director of music and liturgy, began Taizé prayer nine years ago, the service begins with two or three songs that have become familiar to the group. (When a new song is to be introduced, Anderson teaches the music before the service begins.) The songs are followed by a psalm and an Alleluia. All the candles are lighted and there is a reading from Scripture, which varies with the liturgical season. People come forward to place their candles in clay pots around the altar. A period of silence, perhaps ten minutes, follows. During this time, the lighted candles and several large icons provide a visual focus. The group then prays a *Kyrie* for peace and reconciliation. The leader offers general intercessions to which the community responds in song, and the service closes with a sign of peace.

Taizé singing at Ascension includes instrumental accompaniment to the singing. David Anderson says they might use a violin, flute, oboe, perhaps a cello or guitar. Some trained singers also help out. But he quickly points out that Taizé music does not require instruments. "It can be simple or elaborate. You just need solid music leadership—perhaps with a piano or a guitar." Songs at Ascension are sung in several languages that participants might understand—English, Spanish, Italian, and Latin, which is considered a universal language for Taizé prayer. Vicki Tufano says, "The singing is very simple, very repetitive. It invites everybody in and lets you find your own place in it."

The ecumenical prayer service, which started with thirty people, now routinely attracts eight hundred to nine hundred people, some from as far away as Indiana and Wisconsin, and David Anderson has made a special effort to assure that members of other Christian churches in the Oak Park area feel welcome. But Ascension parishioners form the core of the Taizé prayer community, and Anderson says its effects have spilled over into parish meetings. "When we gather in groups, we'll often pray this way."

The depth of the Taizé prayer experience has not been lost on Mickey Wright, another Ascension parishioner. "To say it's spiritual doesn't begin to describe the service. It's peace, it's comfort, it's home. You really belong."

How-To Guidelines

Here are five steps to starting a Taizé prayer service in your parish.

- Learn more about the music and prayer of Taizé. Read some books; order some cassettes or compact discs. (A list of Resources follows.)

- Discuss the idea with the pastoral team and particularly with the music ministers.

- While Taizé singing itself is not difficult, selecting the music, planning the service, and providing gentle unobtrusive leadership does require some liturgical and musical gifts. Be sure that you have access to the talents necessary to do a good job.

- Educate your parish about Taizé prayer—its simplicity, its peace, and its deep Christian roots. Although Taizé prayer is appropriate any time of the year, you might want to introduce it to your parish during Lent or Advent.

• Remember the ecumenical aspect of Taizé and encourage parishioners to invite their friends. Issue a special invitation to the clergy and members of other churches in your area.

Resources

Here is more background information on Taizé community and its music.

• The Taizé Story: The story of the Taizé ecumenical community in France began with Brother Roger, who at first lived alone in the tiny village of Taizé during the early years of World War II. There he prayed three times a day and sheltered political refugees, especially Jews, before he was forced to spend the last years of the war in Switzerland. After the war, he and several other men returned to Taizé where they established a monastic community. The first brothers, including Brother Roger who became prior, were all Protestant. Eventually Catholic men joined them. Today, the brothers come from more than twenty different countries.

The Taizé community welcomes visitors of all faiths from all over the world to their prayer services, and over the years, hundreds of thousands of young people have gathered for prayer in this small village. When Pope John Paul II visited Taizé in 1986, he praised the monks for their ecumenical spirit and the inspiration they provide for young people.

The songs of Taizé, now sung around the world, are memorable—simple phrases repeated in a meditative chant that gradually penetrates the whole person. Brother Roger has written, "Prayer is a serene force at work within human beings, stirring them up, transforming them, never allowing them to close their eyes in the face of evil, of wars, of all that threatens the weak of this world....All who walk in the footsteps of Christ, while being in the presence of God, remain alongside other people as well." (Quotation is from *Songs and Prayers from Taizé* [Chicago: GIA Publications, 1991]), p. 5. More information about the Taizé community can be found at www.taize.fr/en/index.htm.

- Background information and some of the songs of Taizé can be found in the following books from GIA Publications:

  Prayer for Each Day: Taizé, 1998.
  Songs and Prayers from Taizé, 1991.
  Taizé: Songs for Prayer, 1998.
  The Sources of Taizé: No Greater Love, Brother Roger of Taizé, 2000.

  Other items that are also available from GIA Publications are Taizé videos, recordings on cassette and compact disc, and vocal and instrumental music editions. You can reach GIA Publications at 7404 S. Mason Avenue, Chicago, IL 60638. Telephone: 800-442-1358. Web site: www.giamusic.com.

~

Show and Tell Your Family Stories

"Let's celebrate our family histories!" With that brainstorm, which struck in the middle of winter, a small Christian community created a spiritual, fun-filled Family Heritage Picnic for a summer weekend.

One couple in the community had just visited the Ellis Island Immigrant Museum in New York City. Another was immersed in caring for an elderly father. And everyone had children to be nurtured, loved, and guided into or through the teenage years. As they participated in one another's lives, this small Christian community of the Church of the Presentation, Upper Saddle River, New Jersey, sensed an opportunity. The more they talked, the more they realized that past, present, and future were linked and the more they wanted to share—and celebrate—their families' stories.

The group decided to join their celebration with a Fourth of July picnic—intentionally mingling their individual heritages with patriotic themes. The guiding principle for the party became thanksgiving—for family, for country, for friendship with one another, for God's role in all their lives.

Each family was asked to rummage in attics and cellars and closets and select one or two artifacts for a show-and-tell. Each family was also scheduled to bring a favorite main dish or dessert. An informal committee organized the refreshments and also composed a general prayer of thanksgiving.

Before the meal, families briefly described the items they had brought.

There was quite a variety: dog tags fathers had worn in World War II; photographs of grandparents and great-grandparents; hospital bracelets with babies' names; a crucifix from a casket; pictures of first cars; and toy soldiers from a century ago. After the stories, which evoked laughter and a few tears, the group gathered in a large circle. Families offered a short personal prayer of thanksgiving for their own special memories, after which the group prayed together. And then—on to the picnic!

Several years have passed now and the families, both adults and children, still talk about the Family Heritage Picnic. It has provided several families with a comfortable entry into repeated sharing of family memories ("Remember when....") and a valuable way to preserve traditions for the future.

How-To Guidelines

Here are five steps for organizing a Family Heritage Picnic.

- Describe the idea to the small Christian communities or the Core Community in your parish. Solicit their reactions. What modifications to the idea might be necessary? Will each group schedule a picnic of its own, perhaps in a member's yard, or will several groups join together at a common location?

- Decide on a time and place. Check the date with parish, town, and school calendars. Do you want to consider a rain date or a backup indoor location?

- Emphasize the spiritual dimension of the picnic, as well as the food and fun. Make suggestions for artifacts that families might bring. The artifacts could illustrate family memories or they might show our common heritage of faith, for example, a first communion book, a wedding Mass booklet, a baptismal candle, or a statue or picture of a saint most honored by the family.

- Ask for volunteers to take responsibility for planning, for refreshments, for prayer time. (See sample Family Heritage Prayers that follows.)

- Encourage participation by all family members, from the very young to the elderly. You might select a location with ball fields or swimming facilities. Be sure the site is accessible for people with disabilities.

Sample Family Heritage Prayers

For Individual Families

God, our Father, who gave life to each of us
within our own special family,
we thank you for the gift of one another.
We remember those of our grandparents
and great-grandparents and others who have died
(mention by name if you'd like). Pause.
We thank you for the goodness they brought to our family.
We thank you, too, for parents, children, and grandchildren,
for all of us here today.
We pray for all our extended families—aunts, uncles, cousins,
and in-laws (change as appropriate for each family).
Let us always remember where we come from—
and where we are going.
We thank you for the memories of the past that we cherish.
Bless us in the present.
Help us to show your grace to one another,
so your glory may shine ever brighter in our family
and in our world.
We ask this through Jesus Christ, your Son,
in union with the Holy Spirit. Amen.

For the Group

God, our Father, as we gather together in your name,
let us always remember to praise you and thank you.
We thank you for the gift of friendship,
which brings us together.
We thank you for our Church, which holds us together.
We thank you for this opportunity to remember our heritage.
We thank you for the food we are about share,
and for the surroundings in which we celebrate.

We ask your blessing on all the families here,
on all the members of their families.
Help each of us to remember both our family heritage
and our Christian heritage so that we will have the strength
and courage to live out our baptismal promises and to serve you.
We ask this through Jesus Christ, your Son,
in union with the Holy Spirit. Amen.

⌒

Share Spiritual Reading
in Small Groups

Patricia Mahoney says, "Whenever you learn something from a book that helps
you live your life, that's worthwhile." Her parish started a Spiritual Reading
Book Club, transformed it into an Interfaith Spiritual Reading Book Club, find-
ing success with both models.

A few years ago Father Anthony Randazzo, parochial vicar at Notre Dame
Church in North Caldwell, New Jersey, sensed a spiritual hunger in some
members of the parish. Spiritual reading and sharing, he thought, might be one
answer. He initiated a Spiritual Reading Book Club, which met every six weeks.

Patricia Mahoney recalls that Father Randazzo's first selection was Cardinal Joseph Bernardin's book, *The Gift of Peace.* "That really intrigued me,"
she says. "It was such an inspiring book and talking about it with others was
wonderful." She has been a member ever since that first discussion.

Among the other books the club read that first year were *Amazing Grace*
by Kathleen Norris, *Tuesdays With Morrie* by Mitch Albom, and the Book of
Sirach from the Old Testament. Members took turns leading the discussions.
At times, conversation centered on a particularly insightful—or disturbing—
quote from the book. At other meetings, members in the group shared their
own experiences, which were either similar or very different from those described by the authors.

Tuesdays With Morrie was a very popular selection and sparked interest
from neighbors and friends who were members of other religious communities. That led the Notre Dame group to become an Interfaith Spiritual Read-

ing Book Club. Participants now include members of First Presbyterian Church of Caldwell, Congregation Agudath Israel in Caldwell, Caldwell United Methodist Church, St. Aloysius Roman Catholic Church of Caldwell, and St. Peter's Episcopal Church of Essex Fells. Each church group chooses a book, hosts the meeting, and facilitates the discussion for that book.

Recent selections have included *Who Needs God* by Harold Kushner; *Ordinary People As Monks and Mystics* by Marsha Sinetar; The *Song of the Seed: A Monastic Way of Tending the Soul* by Macrina Wiederkehr; and *To Begin Again* by Naomi Levy.

The book club has provided a wonderful way for people of different faiths to share camaraderie and fellowship while at the same time talking about the faith that matters in their lives. The group has often focused on the ways various faiths respond to similar problems. And even when they digress, participants say, the discussions have been lively and enriching. Mary Anne Bainbridge, a member of First Presbyterian Church of Caldwell, says, "It's delightful to be in a group where you can really talk. It helps everyone to deepen their own faith."

How-To Guidelines

Here are six steps for initiating a Spiritual Book Club in your parish.

- Discuss the idea with the parish leadership. Decide on which model would work better for your community: a parish book club or an interfaith book club.

- Place a notice in the parish bulletin and invite interested parishioners to a planning meeting.

- At the meeting, discuss the purpose of a Spiritual Book Club. Is there agreement? Organize the group to select times and places for meeting. Will you need more than one group? Do you want a daytime group and/or an evening one? How many participants in a group? How long are the meetings? How often are they held? How many books will be discussed and over what period of time?

- Consider how the books will be selected. If you have more than one group, do you want to discuss the same book or different ones? You might want to have a short list of books available at the meeting to help groups get started with planning their first discussion.

- In general, try to select books that are available both in paperback and in local libraries. Don't neglect the classics. Many of them, for example, *The Seven Storey Mountain* by Thomas Merton and *The Autobiography of Saint Thérèse of Lisieux: The Story of a Soul,* are readily available in paperback. For purchasing books, you can order copies at local bookstores, at one of the nationwide chains, or from booksellers online.

- Encourage planning ahead for at least six meetings to allow people to get the dates onto their calendars, to obtain copies of the books, to find time to read, to become accustomed to one another, and to ease into discussions.

Resources

Here is more information on some of the specific books mentioned in the article.

- *The Gift of Peace: Personal Reflections* by Cardinal Joseph Bernardin. (Bantam Doubleday Dell, 1998.) Written by Cardinal Bernardin during his final days, the book deals with his life, his faith, and his commitment to living a Christian life in the midst of contemporary challenges.

- *Amazing Grace: A Vocabulary of Faith* by Kathleen Norris. (Riverhead Books, 1999.) A collection of short essays or reflections on familiar religious words such as "grace" and "incarnation." Norris brings history, theology, poetry, and her own deep personal spiritual life to each essay.

- *Tuesdays With Morrie: An Old Man, a Young Man and Life's Greatest Lesson* by Mitch Albom. (Doubleday, 1997.) The true story of the visits the young Albom paid to a dying Morrie Schwartz, a former professor and mentor of the author. Filled with affection and wisdom and good advice.

- The Book of Sirach. Also known as Ecclesiasticus or The Wisdom of Jesus Son of Sirach, it is one of five books from the Old Testament that are known as "Wisdom literature." (The others are Proverbs, Job, Ecclesiastes, and Wisdom of Solomon.) Wisdom literature deals with attaining the good life here on earth and that means having a right relationship with God.

- *Who Needs God* by Harold Kushner. (Pocket Books, 2002.) The famous author of *When Bad Things Happen to Good People* uses the same mixture of wisdom and persuasion as he tackles the subjects of spiritual hunger and religious commitment.

- *The Song of the Seed: A Monastic Way of Tending the Soul* by Macrina Wiederkehr, OSB. (HarperSanFrancisco, 1997.) The author, a Benedictine nun, provides a way to tap into the richness of *lectio divina*, praying with the Scriptures. The book offers a short daily reading and includes guidelines for contemplation, meditation, and journaling.

- *To Begin Again: The Journey Toward Comfort, Strength, and Faith in Difficult Times* by Naomi Levy. (Ballantine Books, 1999.) Rabbi Levy uses personal stories, her own and those of others, as she explores ways to deal with tragedy. She is interested in healing—in showing readers how to seek comfort from others, to repair relationships, to allow themselves to be transformed.

- *The Seven Storey Mountain* by Thomas Merton. (Harvest Books, 1999.) Merton's autobiography remains of deep spiritual interest more than fifty years after it was first published. Merton writes about his early doubts, his conversion to Catholicism, his decision to enter the Trappists.

- *The Autobiography of Saint Thérèse of Lisieux: The Story of a Soul.* Translated by John Beevers. (Image Books, 1987.) Saint Thérèse was only twenty-four years old when she died in 1897, but her book has become a spiritual classic. Her "little way of spiritual childhood" is based on a deep and abiding sense of God's love for each of us; and her message has affected people of every background, age, and intellectual level.

Share Treasured Memories at Wakes

"Remember what great chocolate chip cookies Rita made? She sent boxes and boxes to me at college. Everybody in my dorm used to wait for my mail." Find out how to encourage families and friends to share healing memories at wake services.

Monsignor Jack McDermott, a retired priest from the Archdiocese of Newark, knew the value of storytelling in a community. "Our faith is cemented when we tell our stories," he says. As he ministered at wake services, he began asking, "Does anyone want to say something about the deceased?" He discovered that storytelling under these sad and sometimes stressful circumstances added another dimension to the service and brought a measure of peace to the gathering.

At times of deep sorrow, the ministry of the community is one of companionship to those who grieve. The wake service presents an opportunity for parish ministers to ease the burden of the mourners. The *Order of Christian Funerals* states, "At the vigil the Christian community keeps watch with the family in prayer to the God of mercy and finds strength in Christ's presence" (56).

Customs vary: The core of a wake service might be the recitation of the rosary or it might be a Liturgy of the Word. This would include readings from the Old Testament (particularly the psalms) and the New Testament, followed by a prayer of intercession, including perhaps a litany, the Lord's Prayer, and a final blessing.

Storytelling can be added to either form of a community's wake services. Monsignor McDermott's parish, Church of the Presentation, Upper Saddle River, New Jersey, printed a brochure, "In Memory of You: A Christian Wake Service." In the midst of the readings and prayers, the minister thanks God for the gifts of the deceased and says, "We take this time now to remember these special gifts and cherished memories." The mourners are then invited to "share aloud a treasured memory."

The stories bring laughter and tears and, eventually, acceptance to the mourners. Talking about chocolate chip cookies can also remind us to look for God in the ordinary details of our own lives.

How-To Guidelines

Here are five steps toward encouraging storytelling at wake services in your parish.

- Discuss the idea with the parish team and any other parish members who minister at wake services. Determine their comfort level with the idea.

- Schedule a training session for ministers if you think it would be helpful. Use role-playing to increase comfort levels.

- If your parish does not have a brochure to use for wake services, consider writing one and distributing it to all ministers.

- Be sensitive to the needs and life situations of each family. Encourage ministers to discuss this with the family in early planning conversations for the wake and funeral services.

- Encourage the families to bring appropriate photos and mementos of the deceased to display at the funeral home or the church's gathering space, depending on local customs for wake services. Photographs and treasured mementos can enhance the storytelling.

Stewardship

Share Your Dreams for Your Parish

*W*hen we asked the parishioners to share their dreams with us, it gave all of us a wonderful vision for our community—a sense of who and what we wanted to be." *Father Michael Sheehan, pastor of the Church of the Annunciation, describes how his parish community responded to Dream Sunday.*

On an October Sunday in 1996, Father Michael Sheehan, the recently arrived pastor at Church of the Annunciation in suburban Paramus, New Jersey, distributed a new form to all parishioners. At the top of the page were the words: "It would be marvelous and a great blessing for Annunciation Parish if someday…" Everyone was asked to complete the sentence with his or her own dreams for the parish. The sheets were collected and collated, and on the following Sunday, Father Sheehan distributed a list of the top five dreams:

It would be marvelous and a great blessing if someday…

- the spiritual life of our parish included opportunities for a variety of prayer experiences that met the needs of the diverse groups of people in our community.

- our parish was financially secure.

- the community life of our parish included opportunities for a variety of experiences for our people to meet, to socialize, and to get to know one another.

- the restoration of our church was realized.

- the liturgical life of our parish truly energized us each week to become what we receive: the Body of Christ alive in the world.

111

Father Sheehan is quick to point out that the idea of a Dream Sunday did not originate with him. He attended pastoral training at the National Pastoral Life Center and listened as Father Douglas Doussan, one of the presenters, described how Dream Sunday had worked for him. (More information about the National Pastoral Life Center is available in the Resources section that follows.) But Father Sheehan is also quick to express his enthusiasm for the wonderful response from Annunciation parishioners. The following year, the parish embarked on an ambitious building project that included renovations to both the church and school buildings. Father Sheehan built on the openness people showed after Dream Sunday and involved the entire parish in a year-long process of learning together, of asking and answering questions and, finally, of making decisions as a community.

"When I came to Annunciation," he says, "many retirees were selling their homes and moving away. Many young people moved in. The parish has grown and changed and it was so important to get new people involved." Parishioner Ray Magner agrees. "People will become involved if they feel their thoughts and feelings are being recognized."

Five years after Dream Sunday, Father Sheehan believes Annunciation is well on its way to fulfilling its five dreams. The restored and renovated parish church was dedicated in April 2000, and both the pastoral team and the parishioners are working hard to finish paying off the debt. They have added morning prayer, sung vespers, and a Monday novena to their parish prayer experiences. There are numerous new opportunities for parishioners to meet and get to know one another. The liturgical life of the parish is energizing the community, Father Sheehan says, but he would like to continue to develop this dream.

Parishioner Evey Johnson sums up: "Sharing our dreams has made a tremendous difference in this parish."

How-To Guidelines

Here are five steps you can take to initiate a Dream Sunday in your parish.

• Discuss the idea with the pastoral team. You may also want to involve other parish ministers. The process should be, at every level, consultative.

- Announce and describe Dream Sunday in the parish bulletin for several weeks before the actual date.

- Be sure you have volunteers lined up to distribute the "Dream" forms, then collect them, and collate them. Commit to having the pastoral team read everyone's dreams before the final selections are made.

- Distribute a list of the top five dreams as quickly as possible. Publicize them in the parish bulletin. In working with the final list, you may need to combine various expressions of a similar dream into one final inclusive version. For instance, individual dreams of "parish Taizé prayer" and "novenas" and "monthly Benediction" could be combined into "more opportunities for a variety of prayer experiences."

- Schedule follow-up discussions about the dreams. How will your community make each dream a reality? Involve as many parishioners as possible in small-group meetings, in ministry or liturgical planning sessions, and in prayer for the fulfillment of the parish's dreams.

Resources

- The National Pastoral Life Center has, since 1983, served "the leadership of the Church's pastoral ministry, particularly in parishes and diocesan offices." The Center distributes books, papers, and pamphlets, and publishes *CHURCH*, a quarterly magazine. It also offers workshops and presentations; sponsors symposia, training programs, and conventions; and offers consulting services.

More information is available from the National Pastoral Life Center, 18 Bleecker Street, New York, NY 10012-2404. Telephone: 212-431-7825; fax: 212-274-9786. Web site: www.nplc.org; e-mail: nplc@nplc.org.

What Is a Penny Worth Today?

Several years ago at St. Mary's Church on the Lower East Side of Manhattan, the liturgy committee was searching for a way to draw attention to Stewardship Sunday. They found their answer in the gospel text, "Jesus said to them, 'Give to the emperor the things that are the emperor's, and to God the things that are God's'" (Mk 12:17).

The committee exchanged ten dollars from church funds for a thousand pennies and at every Mass on Stewardship Sunday the committee gave a penny to each person who came into the church. The pastor, Monsignor Neil Connelly, drew out the message in his homily. "Take this penny," he said, "and put it someplace where you can see it often. Let it remind you to give back to God all that God has given you." The church was investing in them, he explained, just as God had done. He asked that they respond by sharing their own time, talent, and treasure.

The message did not go unheeded. St. Mary's saw results spiritually as parishioners tried to deepen their prayer lives. Others became more interested and involved in parish activities or they joined a small Christian community. Collections increased. As one visitor to the parish explained, "There are many poor people here. Many of them live in subsidized housing. A coin is a potent symbol. I saw many smiles that day and I think the penny made them keep on thinking about God and their Church, too."

She continued, "As for me, that liturgy changed the way I look at a penny. It's the least of our coins, but for me the penny has become a reminder to pray."

How-To Guidelines

Here are four steps you can take to make a Penny Sunday work in your parish.

- Initiate a discussion with your pastor, the liturgy planning committee, and/ or the stewardship team several months before Stewardship Sunday. Discuss the symbolism of the penny and its connection to the gospel message.

- Ask yourselves: Is this symbol appropriate for our community? Does it conflict with other messages? How will it fit with the other components of our stewardship campaign?

- Develop materials to explain the message you want to convey. Write something for the parish bulletin. Think about distributing a flyer after Mass. Have someone present an explanation before the liturgy begins and/or be sure that all homilists understand the concept and are prepared to include a reference in their homilies.

- Assign responsibility for getting pennies from a bank and have volunteers at each church door to distribute the coins at each Mass. This could be a good activity for members of small Christian communities, strengthening their own commitment to stewardship and giving increased visibility to the idea of small Christian communities in the parish.

◇

Caring for God's Creation

"We do this because we believe we are meant to care for the earth as God would." St. Mary's Church in Colts Neck, New Jersey, offers an exciting Environmental Expo once a year and that weekend all the Sunday liturgies reinforce the spiritual dimension of the theme.

It has been seven years since St. Mary's Church started an Environmental Ministry. In that time they have developed a number of projects, including a butterfly garden and a water-testing program. Every year, as a major educational effort, the parish sponsors an Environmental Expo in the parish hall and highlights the theme of God's creation in all the liturgies of that day.

The Expo, set up like a science fair, draws on community resources and encourages interaction between parishioners and the exhibitors. Among the exhibits at this year's Expo were booths to learn about composting, environmental-friendly gardening, soil conservation, rescued and rehabilitated wildlife, backyard birding, and energy conservation.

Parishioners enjoying the Expo had already participated in the eucharistic liturgy in which the spiritual dimension of caring for the environment was explored in the homily, in the prayer of the faithful, and in the offertory procession.

At each liturgy the homilists, preaching from the lectionary readings of the day, made connections between the gospel and our obligation to care for the world around us. Such connections can be made with a variety of gospel readings.

Often we find Jesus outdoors pointing to the lilies of the field, sitting in fishing boats on the water, teaching crowds on the hill, or retreating alone to a mountain to pray. Moreover, we are told to follow Jesus.

The petitions of the prayer of the faithful, which were prepared by parishioner Maria Savoia, the founding chairperson of the Environmental Ministry, also highlighted the theme. Here are some examples:

"For this world around us that cries out to God with joy, may its well-being be ensured by our tender care, we pray to the Lord." Response: *"Lord, hear our prayer."*

"For the leaders of our nation, that they might count among their responsibilities an outlook of protectiveness toward the environment, we pray to the Lord." Response: *"Lord, hear our prayer."*

"For the church, that we might model the courage of the apostles and speak out in defense of the earth, we pray to the Lord." Response: *"Lord, hear our prayer."*

"For our St. Mary's community, that we will continue to grow in our appreciation of, and gentle care for, the beauty that surrounds us, we pray to the Lord." Response: *"Lord, hear our prayer."*

Because St. Mary's is located near the ocean, their gifts reflected their particular habitat. At the time of the offertory procession, in addition to the bread and wine, parishioners also presented a bowl of sand, some shells, and a bottle of water from the sea. The lector read the following words:

"Today we offer...

...sand from the shore, a place of reflection that rewards us with gifts of the sea and reminds us of Jesus' call, 'Come and eat.'

…shells, rounded stones, and coral, freely given, for us to ponder the creative and generous spirit of God.

…sea water, teeming with life and beauty and diversity, generously God-given, for humanity to treasure."

ADAPTED FROM WORDS COMPOSED BY MARIE SAVOIA,
ST. MARY'S CHURCH. USED WITH PERMISSION.

In our busy lives, our appreciation of God's creation can become routine. By linking the spiritual dimension of the message with practical activities, St. Mary's reminds its parishioners of the importance of gratitude to God and of caring for God's creation. The benefits of Environmental Sunday go far beyond the day and the place, lasting into the months that follow and rippling out into town, county, and state.

How-To Guidelines

Here are five steps to organizing an Environmental Sunday in your parish.

- Consult with the parish leadership team and with representatives from the ministries of liturgy and social justice.

- Determine the form your event will take. Consider the size of your facilities and the lifestyles of your parishioners. Find a way to celebrate your community's particular environment, be it urban, suburban, or rural. To adequately reflect the topic, be sure to include both the spiritual dimension and the practical or active dimension.

- Delegate responsibilities. Who will contact agencies and non-profit organizations in the area and ask for their participation? Who will handle the necessary arrangements such as set-up and cleanup? Who will guide the liturgical development of the theme?

- Solicit volunteers. In particular, look for ways to involve the children and young people of the parish.

- Schedule the event far into the future. Plan in the fall, for example, for a spring or summer Expo.

Do the Right Thing

Tom Pieters, chair of the finance council at Spirit of Christ Church in Arvada, Colorado, says, "We're in the midst of a building campaign, but we still tithe 14 percent of our income. It's the right thing to do." This parish encourages stewardship and gives away more than $240,000 a year.

Walk into Spirit of Christ Church, in Arvada, Colorado, and look up. On a high beam above the altar you will see a crystal bowl. The bowl is filled with stewardship pledges—commitments of time, talent, and treasure promised to God during the current year. No one sees the contents of the bowl, but members of this parish take their commitments so seriously that the church is now able to tithe 14% of its income to outreach programs. This year Spirit of Christ is donating more than $240,000 a year to non-profit agencies that perform a variety of works of mercy.

Their stewardship program actually began in 1974, the year the parish began. The parish council decided the community needed "to walk the talk." They began by giving away 2 percent of the parish's income. At the same time, they began teaching from the pulpit on the meaning of stewardship. Their program evolved into a three-Sunday effort each fall, much like other stewardship programs. (Some sources of information on Stewardship are listed in the Resources section that follows.) The parish has also created a meaningful community ritual for their giving.

On the third Stewardship Sunday, just after the homily, parishioners receive a stewardship card. Each card has a perforation down the center. Parishioners fill out both sides. One side they keep at home to remind them of their pledge; the other half is brought up at the offertory and placed in the crystal bowl. The bowl remains in view above the altar until the next year when those pledge cards are burned and a new pledge year begins. No one ever sees what is written on the cards. That, the parish council says, is between each person and God.

How does Spirit of Christ distribute the funds? First, the parish determines its annual budget. Whatever remains each year is considered gift—to be donated. Recipients are divided into three categories—local, national, and international non-profits—and each category receives approximately one-third of the available funds. In September, organizations that wish to be considered for funding are asked to apply by providing background information about their work and their budgets.

The ministry responsible for distributing the parish's annual gifts is composed of representatives from various outreach ministries, the finance committee, and the pastoral council. The group meets and considers each application individually and in alphabetical order. Cathi Politano, a pastoral associate, facilitates the discussion, and decisions are made by consensus voting. In a recent outreach budget, of the sixty-six organizations that applied, funds were granted to thirty-six. The grants ranged from $720 to $36,000. All budget figures are published annually in the parish bulletin.

Spirit of Christ followed its initial inspiration. Parishioners "walk the talk" and their sacrificial giving has indeed made a difference—not only in the lives of community members, but also in the lives of many thousands of others who are helped by the agencies that Spirit of Christ helps.

How-To Guidelines

Here are five ways to set up a Tithing Ministry in your parish.

- In budget discussions with the finance committee and the parish leadership determine what percentage of its income the parish wishes to tithe.

- Present the proposal to all the members of the parish and ask for their prayers and their participation. If yours is already a stewardship parish, combine the message with Stewardship Sign-up Sunday. If you are not, you may want to obtain information on stewardship. (Some suggestions appear in the Resources section that follows.)

- Decide how you will distribute funds. Contact non-profit organizations that may need support, and invite applications.

- Encourage participation of all outreach ministries in any decision-making process.

- Commit to total accountability for the funds and the process. Expect success. Pray for it.

Resources

Here are some sources for information about stewardship.

- First, contact your diocesan archdiocesan office to see what information and assistance they can provide.

- The United States Conference of Catholic Bishops (USCCB) has published an excellent pastoral letter that explores the challenges of the Christian's call to discipleship. Its goal is to help Catholics see stewardship as their response to God's gifts. "Stewardship: A Disciple's Response" (May 1993) is USCCB publication No. 567-4 and can be ordered by phone at 1-800-235-8722 or online at www.usccb.org/publishing/stewardship.htm.

- The USCCB also offers other stewardship materials. Among them: *Stewardship and Development in Catholic Dioceses and Parishes: Resource Manual.* This is meant to be used in conjunction with the pastoral letter described above. It provides practical suggestions and step-by-step guidelines for implementing stewardship programs. It is publication No. 5-132 and can also be ordered by phone or online, as above.

- Another Web site on stewardship to consult: International Catholic Stewardship Council at www.catholicstewardship.org.

~

Many Voices, One Sunday Bulletin

"The Body of Christ has many voices," commented a visitor to the Church of St. Joseph in Mendham, New Jersey. Read how the pastor of this suburban church empowers parishioners to spread the Good News in the Sunday bulletin.

Monsignor Kenneth Lasch believes that his is not the only voice that should be heard in the parish bulletin every Sunday. He invites deacons, ministry leaders, and various parishioners to take turns writing the weekly front-page reflection.

Jean and Jerry Jabbour, a recently married couple, were invited to share their insights into the early years of marriage. In their article, "Marriage Is for Keeps," they wrote, "We have found that being proactive in our faith and church community has brought us closer together as a couple by giving us precious time together, while working as a team to benefit others." They reflected on how difficult it is for young couples to find time to nurture a relationship, and how they treasured the "couple time" their work with the religious education team and the youth group provided, especially leading teens on a winter camp weekend. Even the assignment to write an article for the parish bulletin helped them build their identity as a couple and deepened their relationship. "Writing down our thoughts gave us an opportunity to reflect on how we're doing together and on how significant the marriage commitment really is," Jerry says.

Kevin MacKinnon, a fifth-grade religious education teacher, reflected on the gifts of the Holy Spirit, tying his classroom experience with the Scripture readings for that particular Sunday. Mark and Deb Servodidio reflected on the "new beginnings" they've experienced since the birth of their fourth child. "Our new beginning has helped us identify what matters most, which ultimately is time. Time with each other and time with the Lord."

In his article, entitled "From Feast to Feast," Nick D'Amato reflected on the ways the Holy Spirit motivates so many people to work together for the success of the annual parish party on the feast of St. Joseph. Nick describes himself as a "nuts-and-bolts person" but in writing the reflection, he says he began to understand that "something else—the Holy Spirit" was behind all preparations. "How else can you explain the enthusiasm and dedication demonstrated year after year by a variety of folks?"

Monsignor Lasch selects appropriate topics and gives participants plenty of time to think, to pray, and then to write their reflection. He asks for written texts a week or so before the final bulletin deadline so he has time to read them before publication. And he reserves a few weeks in each year for sharing his own thoughts with the community at St. Joseph's.

Parishioners believe they are far richer for having heard many voices speaking through their Sunday bulletin. Each week a copy of the bulletin goes to the bishop, and he has been known to write a note of appreciation for a particular reflection.

How-To Guidelines

Here are five ways to encourage other voices to contribute to your Sunday bulletin.

- Consult with the parish leadership team. Ask for suggestions for contributors and for topics.

- Draw up guidelines for the reflections. Do you want them tied to the weekly Scripture readings? Do you want them to explore ministries or sacraments? Who will select topics and assign to specific people?

- Supply a word limit and offer your assistance with background reading, if help is requested or is necessary.

- Plan far ahead and establish realistic but firm deadlines.

- Write thank-you notes.

∞

Renew the Waters of the Earth

Ask John Dabrowski from St. Mary's Parish, Colts Neck, New Jersey, why he and other parishioners monitor the quality of water in nearby brooks and ponds. The answer is simple yet profound. John says, "It's part of our spirituality. We are stewards of the earth."

Many small brooks and streams and ponds surround St. Mary's Church in central New Jersey, and local residents are proud of their environment. But they are also concerned about the quality of their waters. Fifteen members of the parish have made stewardship of these waters a priority in their Environmental Ministry; they have joined with other local groups to monitor the quality of the water in local streams and ponds.

One Saturday a month, volunteers from St. Mary's visit twelve different locations to collect water samples. They return to the parish hall where they scientifically test the samples, using a variety of chemicals. As part of its work, the group tests for dissolved oxygen, turbidity, nitrates, acidity, and phosphates; these are indicators of healthy or unhealthy water. The results are noted on field data sheets, which are then sent to the county water quality testing program. Monmouth County could not afford to run this program without volunteer help.

St. Mary's volunteers have committed to stay with the testing program for five years, the amount of time the county needs to collect sufficient data to identify the sources of the pollution. They received a grant from the Environmental Justice Program of the United States Conference of Catholic Bishops. (Information about the Environmental Justice Program, including its educational materials and its regional environmental grants program appears later.) They also received support from parish funds and from Clean Communities, a government-sponsored project. By working as volunteers for that effort, they pick up roadside litter along several streets in their community, and in exchange they receive chemicals that they need for testing the waters.

In addition to their monthly testing sessions, the group, which includes a few engineers and an environmentalist, is committed to educating the parish and the local community about the pollution of the local drinking water supply. They also want to encourage parishioners to monitor and alter their behavior to prevent water pollution. With some of the USCCB grant money they received, they distributed more than two thousand copies of a New Jersey Department of Environmental Protection brochure explaining nonpoint source pollution. Nonpoint source pollution—or "people pollution"—is the contamination of our waters resulting from our everyday activities. The brochure suggests ways ordinary citizens can make a difference.

Testing the Waters is a project of St. Mary's Environmental Committee. Their mission, as described in the parish handbook, is "to be an informed channel through which all persons come to recognize that they are called by God to heal and preserve all life on earth as they make choices and take actions to benefit creation now and in the future." Other projects sponsored by this ministry include planting and maintaining a butterfly garden, beach cleanups, recycling collections, and an environmental expo and liturgy. (See page 115.)

How-To Guidelines

Here are seven steps to initiate an Environmental Ministry in your parish.

- Educate yourself about environmental issues that affect your parish. Where can you make a difference? Immerse yourself in the scriptural texts on which our Christian commitment to cherish all creation is based.

- Share your insights with the pastoral team, the social justice ministry, religious education teachers, and any other parish committees or individuals who might be interested. Listen to their responses.

- Order materials on the subject for your parish from the United States Conference of Catholic Bishops. Use the materials for small group discussions. (A list of resources follows later.)

- Use *Beginnings: Human and World Issues (Session 8: One Sacred Community)* or *Embracing Life (Session 5: Ecological Responsibility)* from the RENEW IMPACT Series as an aid for faith-sharing in small Christian communities or small parish discussion groups. Order copies from RENEW International, 1232 George Street, Plainfield, NJ 07062-1717, by phone at 1-888-433-3221, or online at www.renewintl.org/Resources/Pages/faithshare.html.

- Select an issue to which the entire parish can be committed. Prayer, education, and action should be integral to any initiative you choose.

- Draw up a realistic action plan, using the gifts present among your parish community. If you wish, join with neighboring parishes, your diocese, local non-profit organizations, or governmental agencies engaged in environmental work you support. Create your own coalition to address a problem.

- In your organizational efforts, reach out to a broad range of volunteers. Include teens, young adults, and retirees. Be sensitive to time constraints and allot tasks wisely.

Scriptural References

Here are just a few of the many scriptural references you might want to use for prayer and reflection as you consider an Environmental Ministry for your parish.

- Genesis, Chapters 1 and 2. The Creation story. "God saw everything that he had made, and indeed, it was very good" (1:31).

- Genesis 9:9–17. God's covenant with Noah. "I have set my bow in the clouds, and it shall be a sign of the covenant between me and the earth" (verse 13).

- Psalm 104. A song of praise to God the Creator and Provider. "O LORD, how manifold are your works" (verse 24).

- Matthew 6:26. Part of the Sermon on the Mount. "Look at the birds of the air; they neither sow nor reap nor gather into barns, and yet your heavenly Father feeds them."

- John 1:1–3. "All things came into being through him, and without him not one thing came into being" (verse 3).

- Colossians 1:15–20. "He is the image of the invisible God, the firstborn of all creation…" (verse 15).

Environmental Protection Ideas

Each one of us, whether we know it or not, contributes to nonpoint source pollution through our daily activities. As a result, nonpoint source pollution is the biggest threat to many of our ponds, creeks, lakes, wells, streams, rivers, bays, groundwater, and the ocean.

But there is good news. In our everyday activities, we can stop nonpoint source pollution and keep our environment clean. Simple changes in our daily lifestyle can make a tremendous difference in the quality of our water resources.

Here are some ways you can help.

Litter: Place litter, including cigarette butts and fast-food containers, in trash receptacles. Recycle as much as possible.

Fertilizers: Avoid overuse and do not apply them before a heavy rainfall.

Pesticides: Use alternatives whenever possible. If you must use a pesticide, follow the label instructions carefully.

Motor oil: Do not dump used motor oil down storm drains or on the ground. Recycle by taking it to a local public or private recycling center.

Pet waste: Pet owners should use newspaper, bags, or scoopers to pick up after pets and dispose of wastes in the garbage or in the toilet.

Septic systems: Avoid adding unnecessary grease, household hazardous products, and solids to your septic system. Inspect your tank annually and pump it out every three to five years depending on its use.

- This information, all of which is available to the public, was distributed by the New Jersey Department of Environmental Protection (DEP) in a brochure, "Nonpoint Source Pollution." Contact your own state DEP to find out if they publish similar materials.

Resources

- The United States Conference of Catholic Bishops (USCCB) launched its Environmental Justice Program in 1993. The purpose of the USCCB program is "to help educate and motivate Catholics to a deeper respect for creation and to engage parishes in activities aimed at dealing with environmental problems, particularly as they affect the poor." For more complete information, including an overview of their programs, go to www.usccb.org/sdwp/ejp/index.htm.

- A wide range of resources for parishes is available from the USCCB Environmental Justice Program. A complete resource in a single book, *And God Saw That It Was Good: Catholic Theology and the Environment*, includes articles on Scripture, liturgy, and ethics, as well as the full text of important environmental messages from Pope John Paul II and the U.S. Catholic Bishops.

- You can purchase individual copies of Pope John Paul II's message by ordering "The Ecological Crisis: A Common Responsibility." Individual copies of the U.S. Catholic Bishops' letter, "Renewing the Earth: An Invitation to Reflection and Action on Environment in Light of Catholic Social Teaching" can also be purchased.

- There are three parish resource kits, varying both in content and price. All include practical suggestions for parish initiatives. Make your choice based on the full descriptions of content, which appear on the USCCB Web site.

- There are two videos. *Hope for a Renewed Earth* runs sixty minutes and includes both a documentary and a panel discussion. *The Earth Is the Lord's* runs just thirteen minutes and includes a discussion guide.

- You can order any of these resources by calling the USCCB Office at 1-800-235-8722. For more information on all these resources go to www.usccb.org/publishing/environment.htm.

- Small grants to parishes, such as the one received by St. Mary's, are no longer available, but the USCCB Environmental Justice Program does offer regional grants of $4,000 to $6,000 to dioceses that link together to develop local and regional environmental policy agendas. To obtain more information about the grants program and an application form, go to www.usccb.org/sdwp/ejp/samreggrant.htm.